Ray Manley's
PORTRAITS & TURQUOISE
of Southwest Indians

TEXT BY:

CLARA LEE TANNER
Professor Emeritus, Anthropology
University of Arizona
Tucson, Arizona

JOE BEN WHEAT
Curator of Anthropology
University of Colorado Museum
Boulder, Colorado

CONTENTS:

Southwest Indians	5
Navajo	27
Zuñi	53
Hopi	73
Santo Domingo	81
"Old Pawn"	91

Francis Denet Tsosie is a 76-year-old Navajo from Chinle, Arizona. Here he is dressed in traditional tribal costume — velveteen blouse set off with concha belt, chunk turquoise and shell bead necklace, and a silver decorated pouch supported by a coin-covered leather band over his right shoulder. A modern bola tie has been added.

The ceremonial headdress worn by Steve Trujillo of San Juan Pueblo is mindful of that worn by the deer dancers. Influences from the north are to be noted in bound hair and of the northeast in the long beads about the neck.

Published by
RAY MANLEY PHOTOGRAPHY, INC.
238 South Tucson Blvd.
Tucson, Arizona 85716

Library of Congress Catalog Card Number 75-38328
Copyright 1975 by: Ray Manley Photography, Inc.
Publisher: Ray Manley Photography, Inc.
Art Director: Stanley Fabe
Typography and Design: Ad/Graphics
Lithography: Shandling Lithographing, Inc.
Separations: Walker Lithocraft, Inc.
Bindery: Roswell Bookbinding
Printed in USA

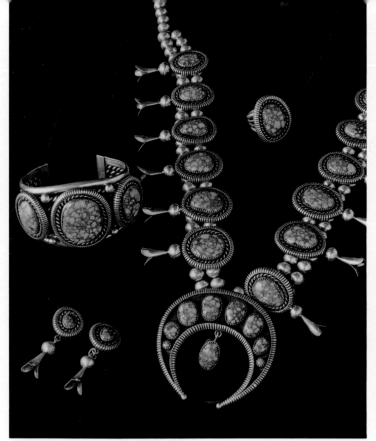

Squash blossom necklace, bracelet and ring, made of Lone Mountain spiderweb turquoise.

Viets Lollahaftewa, Hopi

Publisher's Comments by
Ray Manley

After publishing Ray Manley's *Southwestern Indian Arts & Crafts,* we seriously considered a new publication portraying the great faces of our Southwestern Indians. My son Alan and I began our coverage at the Gallup Ceremonials where a great many of our native Americans gather in August to perform and enjoy the traditional spectacle. I made the arrangements and Alan photographed each face under a wide variety of lighting conditions. We later journeyed to Zuni, Santa Fe Indian Fair, the Rio Grande Pueblos, and the Hopi villages.

After photographing over 100 subjects, I noted that our choices included a wide variety of people with interesting life situations. A handsome Kiowa was in charge of the entire ceremonial program. A fine Navajo man had been in on the landing at Anzio—another was a Navajo code specialist during the same war. A woman with a beautiful beaded neckpiece and strange painted markings on her face was also a gift shop manager near Yuma, Arizona. It turned out that many of these interesting faces were those of Indians well established in the outside world. Some were of highly educated Navajos; a contemporary artist selling his paintings for well over $4,000 apiece and winning awards in Scottsdale as well as Gallup. I remember one face of a beautiful girl with long braids and piercing eyes. She later said she was a breed who had the choice of two worlds. She had chosen that of the Indian world and hoped to better the lives of her people.

We spread proof prints out on a large table and realized we had a great cross-section of today's Indian—a far cry from my original plan. We had envisioned capturing (before it was too late) the strong, lined faces of the old Indian, like Norman Rhodes Gharett and Barry Goldwater had done in beautiful sepia tones in previous years. Weathered faces of the Navajo showed their struggle with the sun and wind. These were great faces that will never happen again, for

the lives of our present generations will not have the mask of hardship seen in the elderly who have survived the rugged outdoor life of the reservations during the past 100 years. (Yes, some are still around and they look just great.)

Nearly every person we photographed wore interesting jewelry and this gave us the point of departure for what we feel is an opportunity to show the reader today's native American and his very best jewelry. We feel that our selection of silver, turquoise and silver, heishi, gold, and other materials can give the reader the opportunity of seeing what authentic Indian jewelry looks like. It can give a standard by which jewelry can be judged.

A telephone call from an irate man from Massachusetts related that much of the jewelry in the East was of questionable quality and why couldn't he buy the fine quality displayed in our previous book and *Arizona Highways.* He had been "ripped off," having paid $1,500 for a necklace worth less than $250. In the first place, there are a limited number of good silversmiths and they can easily sell all they make close to their Arizona or New Mexico homes. Reputable dealers do acquire some of this jewelry and can get it into the distant markets and into the hands of well-known stores. Herein lies the necessity of knowing your dealer. If he is reputable, he will give you a written guarantee of the jewelry's authenticity and be willing to refund your money if he was mistaken.

We hope our combination of the contemporary faces of our Southwestern Indians, and the fine articles about them written by Clara Lee Tanner, as well as the quality reproductions in full page size will give our readers the best insight to date. With the finest selection of good natural turquoise and other jewelry, we hope the impact of near actual-size reproductions will further educate the reader as to the quality detail of the art and the other characteristics of many good kinds of turquoise.

Jewelry designed by Pat Patania. The central pendant utilizes detailed applique
of desert growth, roadrunner, muddancers and other themes to surround the
large Kingman stone. The other pieces are ornamented with the same themes
and use smaller pieces of turquoise, all Persian. These forms illustrate the
influence of Navajo jewelry on the Anglo craftsman.

Southwest Indians

Diverse cultures and diverse men make up the Indian of the southwestern United States today. A long background of hundreds of years, multitudinous ways of life, and a variety of physical types have contributed to these diversities. From the mammoth hunter throwing his atlatl stick to the modern Indian silver craftsman revealing his sophisticated abilities in an exquisitely delicate creation is a long path travelled by these men. Through the centuries, even the millennia, they have struggled ever upward. They have lived and loved, they have succeeded and failed, they have felt keen deprivation and have known the joys of fulfillment, they have warred and known peace. All of this is registered in their cultures and their countenances.

The old ways linger in far corners, but the modern world has caught up with many of these Indians. Tribal centers buzz with activities—with everything from council meetings and busy craft guilds to the publication of newspapers and dispensing of gasoline. In their appearance, some Indians look like a breath out of the past, wearing hair-do, dress, and mocassins long since outmoded by some tribal brothers; others, very much of the present, are dressed in up-to-the-minute business suits. Elderly men and women with seamed faces but smiling eyes speak in the native tongue to young people just home from college, the past mixing with the present.

Too, the craft of jewelry expresses the past and the present. Turquoise and shell reflect continuity out of prehistoric years; silver attests to more than a hundred-year contact with Europeans. Styles and designs reveal a continuing creativity as well as a response to the whims of other Indians and white men alike.

A closer look at these trends will help to better understand the Indian countenance and what has transpired in jewelry of the Indian world today.

Cultural beginnings in the Southwest are vested in a ten thousand or more year history. In earliest years there lived in this area two main types of Early Man—fellows who hunted big game such as the mammoth, and their contemporaries and followers who hunted small animals and gathered grass seed, nuts, and berries. The former contributed much to the perfection of the use and control of the right hand in the production of finely shaped and flaked stone tools. The latter produced smaller and generally not so well-made tools, but, because they frequented caves, they left remains which tell of their developments in basketry, shell jewelry, and other crafts. It is likely that most, if not all, of these accomplishments carried on into later years.

Coming after Early Man were sedentary populations. These latter folk gradually developed from simple corn cultivation to a more extensive agricultural base, with beans and squash and irrigation systems. As a consequence there developed larger villages and more complex social organization. The crafts inherited from Early Man were carried to greater heights and new ones were invented.

Some cultural variations occurred in different parts of the Southwest. This can be simply presented in terms of three major cultures, what they accomplished, and their relationship to later, historic tribes. The states involved in this include Arizona, New Mexico, Colorado, and Utah, with some slight overlapping into adjoining areas. In the northern portion, and centering where these four states meet, were located the Anasazi people; to the south and southwest were the Hohokams; and to the south and east were the Mogollones. At times these people mixed or exchanged ideas.

Anasazi homes moved through the centuries from pit houses excavated into the ground to pueblos; the latter were large multi-storied apartment-like houses which accommodated the entire village. Hohokam peoples lived in relatively shallow pit houses most of their prehistoric years. Pit house to pueblo was also the story of the Mogollones, with the latter rather smaller and of only one or two stories. All of these people raised corn, beans, and squash; some puebloans depended on rainfall for cultivation while others, and the Hohokams, developed irrigation systems. It is possible that chiefs or like headmen were village leaders; it is likely that a religious connection was strong, whatever type of rule prevailed.

All of these people produced whatever they needed. This may explain in part the high levels of accomplishment which prevailed in all of the crafts, in basketry, textile weaving, pottery, jewelry, and several additional expressions.

Jewelry was developed out of available materials at hand, such as colored stones, clay, bone, wood, and a few others, plus shell which was largely imported from the Gulf of California and some from the West Coast. Turquoise and shell were favored above all other materials. Many techniques of working were devised, particularly for shell and stone, all to be inherited by the historic Indians. These included cutting, breaking, abrading, incising, carving, and drilling; some painting was done on shell, some stones were inset into the same material, and much mosaic was done. A variety of objects was produced, including rings, bracelets, necklaces, and earrings. Even nose and lip plugs were made and worn!

Camilio Tafoya, born in Santa Clara Pueblo, has long practiced pottery making. He was introduced to the world of clay when he was a child, helping his mother, Serafina. Later he worked with his wife Agapita, a common practice among Pueblo potters. For a time, Camilio was interested in horse sculpture. Now, "73 years young," he features smaller-sized vessels, and decorates them with prehistoric pottery designs.

The Anasazi are acknowledged as the ancestors of the contemporary pueblo Indians, the Mogollones are thought to have contributed some blood to the puebloid lines, and the Hohokams are thought to have been the ancestors of the Pimas and Papagos. This means, of course, that all of the historic Southwestern peoples were of mixed blood. Basically they were Mongoloid, but even the first arrivals, the Big Game hunters, may well have had some other strains in their blood before they began to migrate across

the Bering Straits into North America. Later arrivals, still in prehistoric times, probably added to this mixture. Historically other additions have been made to the Indian blood lines, including, among others, Spanish, Mexican, and a variety of Anglo types. Slight wonder that one sees tall and short Indians, varying shades of skin color, high cheek bones and a lack of the same, the Mongoloid "dish face" or straighter lines in the face, light body and facial hair, and a variety of body proportions. Predominant still, are the straight black hair and the fine dark eyes. Non-southwestern Indians have played a part in the mixture also, as is to be seen in the tall stature of the Taos people who have mixed with the Plains Indians.

Historically, there are two main groups of Indians in the Southwest—the puebloans and the non-puebloans. In the first are included all of the tribal villages of the Rio Grande drainage of New Mexico, among others, northernmost Taos, and, south along this river, Santa Clara and San Ildefonso, Tesuque, Cochiti, Santo Domingo, Jémez, and Acoma. To the west and still in New Mexico is Zuñi, and on into northern Arizona the Hopi villages. Non-puebloans include the Apaches and Navajos, both late arrivals in the Southwest (but still here several centuries before Spaniards came), and all the Yuman tribes. Most of the latter live along the Colorado River, although several of these groups have moved into the interior of Arizona. Around the turn of the century a few Yaquis from Mexico settled in southern Arizona.

The many puebloan tribes have carried on native culture in varying degrees. At Taos two large pueblo units have survived, while at Zuñi, individual houses are rapidly replacing the older architectural style. Home furnishings reflect the history of the area, from Spanish fireplaces to gas stoves, from benches to overstuffed sofas. Dress, too, is extremely varied. Old styles, some going back into pre-history, are worn, largely in ceremonies. Remnants of Spanish influence are obvious in embroidery hanging down at the bottom of the skirt; at the opposite extreme is the business suit, the mini skirt, or long formal dress. Remnants of buckskin clothing are to be found in various situations, for example, in the leggings with side fringes worn by the Taos Indian. Plains Indian influences are to be noted in a variety of details, in bead work, in great head-pieces, in feather bustles.

Religion has remained a cementing factor in puebloan life, serving to preserve many of the old ways. Many cere-monies continue deep in channels of the past, from the organization of the rite itself to costumes, headgear, masks. To be sure, new materials may be substituted, then again tradition may dictate the handwoven cotton fabric for the Hopi kilt, the shoulder blanket. Decorative patterns on the garments, designs on the mask may, in some instances, compare favorably with those found in prehistoric examples. Undoubtedly many of the religious concepts are deeply rooted in the past. Yet, in the same village where the past is held so vital to proper functioning, the present may be called upon for an important part of the way of life: earning a livelihood. The man who dances in a sacred performance one night may return to his salary-earning job the next day, performing duties under circum-stances as modern as tomorrow.

The old theocratic rule in puebloan villages has given way to tribal councils or, in the Rio Grande, to an all-pueblo council. Like the organization itself, the duties performed by the group are concerned with problems unheard of in the native situation. Rather than family problems, clan lands, the setting of the ceremonial calendar, the council is now involved with road building, a new school, or other formerly unheard-of matters.

Puebloan economy has also become involved in new slants. The age-old, basic produce is still cultivated, but to the threesome—corn, beans, and squash—have been added many products, such as the Spanish-introduced tomatoes, peppers, and wheat, among others. Anglo contacts have been more significant in the addition of new agricultural techniques, with large-scale machinery, fertilization, crop rotation, and such. Much of the latter is taking toll in religion, for many of the religious rites had to do with fertility and growth of the crops. Where there is less modernization of agricultural procedure, there are practiced more of the original rites.

Non-puebloans of many centuries' residence in the Southwest, the Piman and Yuman speaking peoples, present quite a different picture. The Pimas proper have lived along rivers, maintaining a higher standard of living. Permanent villages, irrigation cultivation, more developed arts and crafts have long been their lot. Only when white men cut off their water supply with the building of a dam did their lives change appreciably. The end result has been a terrific loss of native culture and an acceptance of that of the invader. On the other hand, their language brothers to the south, the Papagos, have known hard times since far back into prehistory. Natively, their lives were centered in limited farming in open lands in the spring and summer; then they returned to the mountains to eke out a frugal existence for the rest of the year. Historic contact meant the acquisition of cattle and a more permanent water supply in the form of wells. The rigors of their lives allowed for slight development of the crafts, yet today the Papagos produce the greatest quantity of baskets of any Southwestern tribe. Little survives of their native religion, and less of their aboriginal political organization for they, too, have a tribal council.

Yuman tribes have long had extremely simple social organization and relatively limited material culture. During this century, several of these tribes produced outstanding basketry, such as the Yavapai, Havasupai, and the Walapai. Their simple agricultural and/or stock raising lives have

been ordered by tribal councils. Little remains of their native religion, and today little is produced in the way of crafts.

More vigorous and more numerous are the Apache and Navajo tribes. Both came to the Southwest several centuries before Spanish arrival. Both were semi-nomadic but have settled down into more permanent homes in recent years. Both have strong tribal councils which are greatly concerned with the economic welfare of their people. The fine basketry of the Apaches has dwindled in quantity and quality but it has survived.

Navajos represent the largest of all Southwest tribes, numbering over 140,000. To sheep raising and fly-by-night farming have been added cattle raising and, in some areas, large-scale cultivation. The tribe has developed the first all-Indian-managed college in the country. Their very strong tribal council has extended its interest from the political to education, a tribal museum, construction all over their reservation, a tribal herd of cattle, and many other ventures. It is not surprising that this tribe has perpetuated two of the best known of all Southwestern crafts—rug weaving and silversmithing. Navajos are committed to strong native religious ideals also, particularly in their curing rites which involve beautiful sandpaintings; these represent the purest form of native American Indian art.

Many recent trends have further affected the Indian himself and his jewelry. Mixture of blood continues, particularly as young people from different tribes meet in large schools and marry. Easy travel has beckoned to other tribesmen; for instance a few Sioux and Kiowas now make their homes in the Southwest. And, although distinct tribal styles of jewelry prevail, there is more and more exchange of ideas because of fairs, art exhibits, the Gallup Ceremonials, and other displays which bring Indians together. The current widespread popularity of Indian jewelry is responsible for a terrific increase in quantity, and, to some degree, a decrease in quality. Despite this, much fine jewelry is still produced by Southwest Indians.

Joseph Lonewolf is the son of Camilio Tafoya from Santa Clara Pueblo. Featuring small pieces of pottery, he often depicts single subjects or small scenes of several animals. He is well-known for his sgraffito, a style of carving which reveals several layers of differing colors, thus giving great delicacy and esthetic quality to his ceramics.

Left, Patsy Trujillo (Stone Lake Flower), a Taos Pueblo Indian girl, wears ornate earrings that hang below the shoulder line. Elaborate neckpieces combine round silver and stone beads with elongated dentalium-like beads of Plains style. Patsy began dancing at the age of two and is now a university student.

Adam Trujillo (Red Deer), a Taos Indian, has performed at the Gallup Indian Ceremonials for the 54 years of its existence. Here he is in "full dress" regalia, complete with elaborate Plains' style headpiece.

Ben Marcus, a Taos, New Mexico, Indian man, reflects the almost enigmatic air which frequently surrounds these Puebloans. Wrapped from head to toe in a striped blanket, their physical features (from tall stature to facial outline) reflect Plains contact.

Lori (Flying Eagle) Platero is a Taos Pueblo Indian. Many Plains traits are to be noted in the dress of this Pueblo girl, such as the hair-do and decoration, the beaded garment, and the long beads in the choker.

Acknowledgements:

The jewelry photographed for this book came from Indian art stores and private collections in Massachusetts, California, Oregon, Colorado, Texas, New Mexico, Nevada, and Arizona. We wish to express our deepest thanks to those who mailed us their valuable jewelry or traveled many miles to bring it to us. Thankfully, all was returned without mishap.

Again, we are most deeply grateful to Don and Nita Hoel, for our book's jewelry pages are built around many of their superior pieces. Others whose fine collections helped were: Charles Eagle Plume, Tobe Turpen's Indian Trading Company, Gilbert Ortega's Indian Arts, Half Red Man, Inc., The Eagle Dancer, Gene Landurand, Tanner's Indian Arts, Thunderbird Shop, Kachina Shop, Wise Owl Traders, Apache Turquoise Sales, Rainbow Traders, Hopi Cultural Center, Museum of Northern Arizona Gift Shop, Mr. and Mrs. Albert Cutter, Mr. and Mrs. Francis Feeney, Mr. and Mrs. Edward Masland, Mr. and Mrs. Dennis Lyon, Tin-Nee-Ann Trading Company, B. C. Waddell and Sons, Selser Gallery, Delmar Adams, and Indian Nation Trading Post.

We have withheld the artist's name from each individual piece except where that person's contribution to modern innovation has seemed significant. It is also impossible to identify the maker of each piece as they are not all signed. The following names do represent most of the creators of the fine examples illustrated: Della Appa, Joe Tchethlakai, Paul and Jessie Rosetta, Joe Reano, Charlie Quetauki, Bonnie Quam, Lambert Homer, Thomas Gilbert, Lee Edaakie, Edward Beyuka, Frank Vacet, Dennis Edaakie, Roger Skeet, David Tsikewa, Lavina Tsikewa, Charles M. Yazzie, Lawrence Saufkie, Glen Lucas, Virgil and Shirley Benn, Tom Weakkee, Dixon Shebala, Larry Pinto, Carl Luthey, Ramon Platero, Floating Leaf, Gary Johnson, Phillip Secquaptewa, Duane Maktima, Mary and Lee Weebothey, Fred Peshlakai, Ramon Platero, Warren Analasy, Elliot Qualo, Preston Monongye, Charles Loloma, Frank Patania, and Carlos Diaz.

We are also indebted to the Intertribal Indian Ceremonials at Gallup, New Mexico. Here, during mid-August, one can see the greatest gathering of Indians in the entire country. Other events are the Fourth of July Flagstaff Indian Pow-Wow and the September Navajo Tribal Fair, both offering similar gatherings, and all featuring parades, dancing, rodeo events, and competitive exhibits of the arts and crafts of many Indian artists.

...at Goodnight of Taos, the northernmost of all the Pueblos. Plains
...atures are to be noted in his beaded headband and, above this,
...e natural and dyed porcupine headpiece which falls down to his
...ack. Pat is a very famous Hoop dancer.

Incarnacion Pena, a San Ildefonso, New Mexico, Indian, has been painting for many years. Although he painted very little through the years, he developed a delicacy of style. Pena's fine physical features are duplicated in many Pueblo Indian faces.

Reyes P. Toya, a Jemez Pueblo woman, has been a winner in the "best dressed" contest at the Santa Fe Indian Fair numerous times. Slight wonder, for here she is impeccably dressed in a flowered, Pueblo style garment and is bedecked with a quantity of necklaces — several plain bead, an old squash blossom style, and a coral necklace.

Juan Chavarria has been the governor of his Pueblo, Santa Clara, several times. Several honors have come to Chavarria, among others, the Catlin Peace Award in 1973, the New Mexico Distinguished Public Service Award in 1974, and Man of the Year in 1957 for promotion of the Puyé-Cliff Indian Ceremonial.

Amelia Caster is a Quechan from Ft. Yuma, California. During World War II she was a spot welder with U.S. Steel in Los Angeles. She belongs to a dance group which has appeared at the Gallup Indian Ceremonials since 1967. Currently, she runs a curio shop on the Ft. Yuma Reservation.

Leonard Carlos, an Arizona Pima Indian, is an "old timer" who could probably tell many a tall tale. This tribe has lost most of its native ceremonies and many of its mores, but the knowing look in Carlos' eye tells that his memory is long.

Oren Fulwilder, a Pima Indian of southern Arizona, represents the modern active tribesman who has much to offer his people. Simple reminders of his tribal past are the tie about his head and the decoration on his shirt. The necklace is probably from another tribe.

Caran J. Wells is of mixed descent: Picuris, Cherokee, plus Irish and Spanish. "I'm a breed — just a breed," she says, but her lovely face denies just a breed. Eyes and hair bespeak her Indian heritage; soft, light skin tells of varied grandparents.

The jovial smile of Paul Trujillo of Cochiti Pueblo, New Mexico, reflects the genuine and deep sense of humor possessed by so many of these Indians. Typical of Pueblo Indians, he wears a bit of jewelry, a shell bead and chunk turquoise necklace.

Cloia Moore is a beautiful Sioux maiden who has chosen Arizona for her new home, not unlike thousands of non-Indians seeking the warmth of the Southwest.

Todd Rawlinson, age 12, is a handsome young Sioux Indian living in Phoenix. He wears beautiful beaded pieces, the head band and wide band over his shoulders. About his neck is a choker-type necklace favored by many Plains Indians.

Sam Yazzie is a Sioux living in Chinle, on the Navajo Reservation. He is gaily dressed in elaborate pieces of beadwork with his vest mindful of an old-style floral type. His ornate headband also suggests older styles as does his porcupine quill headpiece. The dark glasses update the young man to the present moment.

Necklaces and bands of various sorts are crafted by the Western Apaches of eastern Arizona. The larger necklace here is of the style worn by young girls at their puberty rites, while the smaller one, of twisted, vari-colored beads and an eagle-decorated pendant as well as the band are made for sale.

Pollen is sprinkled over a young Apache maiden and her godmother during an Apache puberty ceremony.

10

Performers at the Flagstaff All-Indian Pow Wow, these Apaches — drummer, chanter, and crown dancer — may remind us of the colorful past, for the chanter could easily fit into a scene with either Geronimo or Cochise.

APACHE

Carol Jane Burdette, a San Carlos Apache maiden who lives at Peridot on the Reservation, wears the dress and adornment of a young girl at her coming-out ceremony. Buckskin dress and beaded T-necklace are generally worn today. The elaborate head piece is not typically worn at these rites.

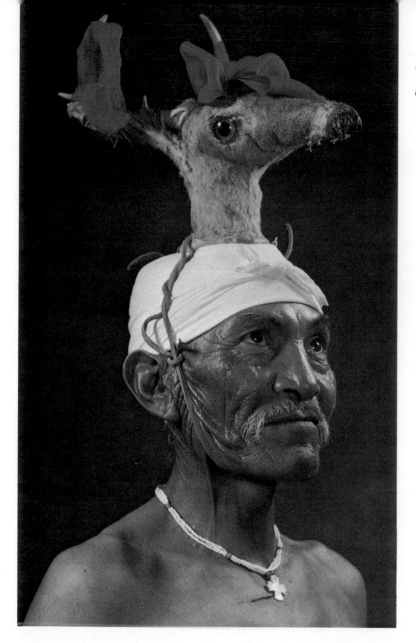

Tanned by many years in the harsh Sonoran Desert sun, this face is that of a Yaqui deer dancer. Ray Manley made this photograph nearly 30 years ago.

Carlos Diaz of Tucson is a native of Colombia, South America. He combines originality, creativity, and a touch of the Indian influence in his jewelry forms, using a variety of stones to enhance them. Both silver and gold are used by this artist. Coral is effectively blended with other materials in all of these pieces. Malachite is added to the choker style necklace, turquoise and shattuckite to the ring. Turquoise only is combined with the coral in the larger, modernistically styled bracelet (right) while all four of these stones, in varied sizes and shapes, are attractively arranged to create the lighter bracelet (left).

Left: Rita Ann Ventura was elected the 1975 Miss Papago and says she represents members of this tribe. A senior in high school, her plans include a college career with a major in nursing. The points of her woven crown are ornamented with miniature Papago baskets.

Tom Manchahty Ware, a young Kiowa-Comanche, has been "dancing since walking" which was when he was about one year of age. He is a member of the oldest Kiowa tribal dance organization and also has his own family dance group. As a musician, a flutist, featuring rock and other types of music, he appears frequently on television and at pow-wows and other shows.

Other Southwestern Tribes

Bill Tallbird, a Cheyenne tribesman, now lives in Gallup, New Mexico. He wears a modern version of a Plains style necklace of long white beads (often of bone), alternated with small metal beads.

21

Pattie Aitson is a sister of Clarice (right). She is also in high school in Gallup, New Mexico, and a member of the school band. She has performed with a Kiowa dance group for about six years.

Freda Jo Tapedo is a mixture of Kiowa-Apache and Seminole now living in Oklahoma. She was Sequoya Intertribal Princess in 1975, and for the same year, Miss Weatherford Teen Ager for the State of Oklahoma. Her own tribes honored her for two years, 1974-76, as their Society Princess. Freda is studying ballet.

Lovely Clarice Aitson, a Kiowa-Navajo Indian, is now living in Gallup, New Mexico, where she is a sophomore in high school and very much interested in music. Her black hair is held in place by large beaded barrettes, of a style made by many Indians today. She wears a Navajo silver belt, plus Plains style necklaces.

Lucy Lewis is a most familiar name in the international ceramic world. Now three-quarters of a century old, she has produced some of the finest pottery of the Southwest. Her products have been exhibited in Europe and the Near East, and are in museums and private collections from coast to coast. She has received many honors for her beautiful wares which feature both life form and abstract geometric styles of decoration. In addition to justly earning renown for her ceramics, Lucy Lewis raised a family of nine children.

Rose Gonzales of San Ildefonso is the epitome of sweetness of personality, a trait that is encountered in many Pueblo women. She is an accomplished potter, and has won many awards in competitive exhibits. Retiring and modest, she wears a necklace as classic as her character.

Rio Grande

Margaret Tafoya of Santa Clara Pueblo is matriarch of a fine family of potters. She herself is an outstanding craftsman, having produced pottery of superior quality for years. The gentleness reflected in her face has endeared her to many.

Marie Chino of Acoma is a well-known potter; in this craft she has taken many prizes for her superior designs and workmanship. Although she paints varied shapes in several ways, she is most famous for a geometric style, an example of which she holds in her hands.

Marie C. Herrera, a happy Tesuque Pueblo lady, wears multiple necklaces, as do many Pueblo women, including the traditional shell bead-turquoise style, a heishi, large bead type, and also an unusual three-strand, round turquoise bead type.

Manuelita Fragua is a Jémez Pueblo woman. She wears Navajo style plain silver squash blossom earrings and a necklace of the same type, with a single stone backing of a single blossom, plus a Zuñi style squash blossom necklace, with more turquoise settings. Her smile speaks of the gentleness of these people.

Puebloans

Young as he is, this little fellow is as ready for the dance as any. Most of the beadwork he is bedecked with is modern but recalls earlier styles in some of its designing. His porcupine quill head piece is certainly worn at a rakish angle.

Philip Gover is a Pawnee who lives at Chinle, Arizona. He attended BIA schools and Bacone College. Twenty years later, he took his degree at Oklahoma State University. In the meantime, he had "made initial landings in Sicily and Italy," losing his left arm below the elbow. He has been involved more recently in teaching and guidance.

Anna Mae Bernallie (with the umbrella) and Helen Wauneka are both Navajos who work for ONEO. Helen is employed with Emergency Food and Medical Supplies. Their costumes and jewelry have been traditional in this tribe since the second half of the nineteenth century. Goats and sheep are usually owned by the women in the Navajo tribe.

NAVAJO

Navajos were the first Indians in the Southwest to do any silvercrafting. Whether or not they were the first to do metal work is a moot point, for the Spaniards introduced copper and brass kettles and had some of the Indians, among them the Zuñis, make objects to be worn on the body, to ward off rheumatism. Too, a few Southwest Indians, including the Navajos, wore jewelry of copper and brass, plus a few items of iron, and some of silver, for years before they ever did any metal crafting. One authority says that the Navajos had worn quite a bit of silver for many years before they learned to work it. Bennett quotes a date as early as 1795, stating that Navajo leaders were at this time wearing silver. Further, brass and copper had been and remained popular for many years. In fact, as silver was not too plentiful before and after the turn of the century, Navajos continued to make bracelets from heavy copper wire which they acquired at trading posts. It was a simple matter to pick up a length of the heavy metal wire and twist it into a wearable object.

A Mexican by the name of Nakai Tsosi taught the first Navajo smith, Atsidi Sani, how to work in silver. They had been friends for some years, visiting back and forth, before this came to pass. First, Atsidi Sani learned to work in iron, a craft he then taught to his four sons. One story has it that it was not until after the return of the Navajos from their captivity at Ft. Sumner in 1868 that Atsidi Sani was taught the working of silver. He then taught his four sons this newer craft. These details are from the story of an old Navajo as related to John Adair. It may be added here that there is some evidence that the Navajos could have learned silver crafting as early as the 1850s. After Nakai Tsosi, other Mexicans taught other Navajos, particularly during the 1870s. Silvercrafting was now on its way.

In the beginning, very few men worked at this craft. By degrees it became more widespread, and, as the members of this tribe became more and more interested in possessing and wearing jewelry and trading or selling it, more Indians participated in its production. About 1940, an estimate was made that there were 600 smiths. Certainly the number by the 1970s was legion. Men were the smiths in earlier years, and, reputedly, women did not do any metal craft until about 1900, then largely helping their husbands. By the 1930s there were a few Navajo women independently producing silver work; many more were added to the list by the 1970s. To the Navajos, this craft has never been the chore of an entire family as it was and is among the Zuñis, although husband-wife teams continued to be common.

In early years, the teaching of silvercraft was from one man to another; some Indians contended that it must be from one blood relative to another. This situation began to change with the teaching of this craft in the Indian schools. Beginning in the 1940s, Ambrose Roanhorse was giving instruction in silver working at Ft. Defiance School, with splendid results. This trend continued into the 1970s with silversmithing being taught at the Institute of American Indian Art, Santa Fe, among other places. Some Navajos learned the craft in a white man's shop, rarely from the owner, more frequently from another Navajo, related or not. The "teacher" of this craft, then, has varied greatly through the years. Occasionally a woman is the teacher; there are recorded instances of a wife teaching her husband.

Some think of groups of silversmiths, large or small, working together as a recent development. However, Adair related the case of a Navajo man who, in the early twentieth century, had a silver shop and ten men working for him. With the terrific increase in interest in Indian jewelry in the late 1960s and the first half of the 1970s, this was a common trend. More frequently it was a white man who employed from two to three smiths to as many as forty or fifty.

American silver coins were first used by the Navajo smith, from the beginning of the craft to about 1885. These would be hammered into the shape of the desired piece and then finished with sheers, file, and a homemade blowpipe, the latter for soldering. The second basic method of working silver was casting. A crude mold was cut from a soft rock as an ingot which was roughly in the shape of the desired piece, or sometimes in the form of the actual object. Melting the silver was done in makeshift crucibles, frequently a piece of prehistoric pottery (Navajo pottery was not good enough), using homemade goatskin bellows. In time, all of this crude equipment was replaced by commercial items except for the mold for casting. To this day, a native soft stone is still used with the shape of the piece of jewelry cut into one piece. A second piece of stone is left plain and placed over the first, the two are tied together, and the molten silver is poured into this mold. When the casting is removed, it is a rough, rather unattractive piece. It is now that the Navajo expresses his great interest in and love for silver for he will polish and polish until the metal has a most pleasing surface. Formerly this was done by hand, today it is accomplished on a buffing wheel.

As far as decoration of the earliest pieces is concerned, there was little of it. A cold chisel or a file was used to make straight lines and simple designs; sometimes equally simple elements were scratched onto the silver surface with an awl.

The decorative parts of bridles were probably among the earliest pieces of silver made by Navajos simply because it was the iron workers who made bridles who became the first silversmiths. Bracelets and rings were very early also, for these pieces had been made of copper and worn for years. Conchas for belts were the first pieces made by one old smith (about 1878). An illustration from J. C. Ives, dated 1858, shows a Navajo wearing a heavy dark belt decorated with what appear to be silver conchas. Of course the question arises: were these traded from Plains Indians or were they made by Navajos? Plain beads and najas (crescent-

Little Lynnette Yazzie, a pert Navajo miss from Ft. Defiance, is all of 3½ years old. Lynnette's grandfather learned of this style of war dance costume from Kiowa friends. He formed "The Blue Eagles" dance team, with his two sons and a daughter, which has danced throughout the nation. Little Lynnette keeps up with the family tradition by appearing at the Gallup Intertribal Ceremonials in costume. Lynnette's cousin, Ophelia Yazzie, appears with her in this photo.

shaped pendants) were made not later than the early 1880s, and more likely in the 1870s. A few of these are also recognizable in very early, dated photographs. The squash blossom necklace was later, seemingly developing some time in the 1880s. Actually, this is really a pomegranate blossom, and was not inspired by the squash.

Objects were made into the 1890s which were not produced, or rarely so, thereafter. Among these were little bells hammered out of quarters; as the Navajos disapproved of a woman and her son-in-law meeting face-to-face, she wore this bell to warn him of her approach. Another unusual object was the silver tobacco pouch or canteen, apparently made in the mid-1880s for soldiers; these were difficult to make as they were formed of two domed pieces of silver soldered together, with a neck added. They tended to be made rarely in later years. Long, slender powder horns were also crafted. When no longer needed, and as silver was scarce, these were usually melted down and made into jewelry. Bridles were commonly made during the last years of the nineteenth century; thereafter they were crafted far less frequently. All previously made forms of jewelry continued during this 1885-1900 period.

After 1890 most of the silver work was done in Mexican coins, particularly the "dobe dollars," which were preferred over American silver as they had less alloy in them, and thus were softer. Although one story has it that Navajos began using turquoise in 1880, it is likely that it was sparingly used until the middle of the 1880s or perhaps even until the 1890s. Persian turquoise was introduced to the Navajos as early as the 1890s.

The years 1880 to 1900 are sometimes referred to as the classic period in Navajo silversmithing. Several points which would support this would include the following: Craftsmen had enough experience back of them to enable them to do more finished work. Their natural feeling for original design had reached a first peak in silverwork; some very fine, heavy cast and wrought pieces resulted from a happy blending of artistry, creativity, and developed technology. Much work without stones was featured, such as wide bracelets with one or two design elements carefully stamped on them; some were elegant with more stamping; or heavy, medium width styles with simply filed designs were expressive of creative imaginations. Filing remained popular for many years to come. Another technique which overlaps the late 1800s and earlier 1900s was repoussé, which was productive of raised circles, lozenges, and diamonds on bracelet surfaces. It was often combined with stamping.

There were turquoise-set pieces which represent a peak of Navajo stone work. Some were cruder, for they were set with Navajo cut stones which were often irregular in shape, rougher on the surface, and not too well matched in color; yet they had a charm all their own. Other bracelets were enhanced by well cut and well matched Persian turquoises. If stones were used, often there was a frugal use of other decorative features, thus stressing that wonderful Navajo feeling for setting off the metal in combination with the blue stone. Much of the simplicity of this late nineteenth century work was enhanced by rugged massiveness, these typical Navajo features.

Although the jewelry trade had been brisk between Indians of the Southwest, there was no real commercialization of this craft until 1899. At this date the Fred Harvey Company sent a representative with turquoise and silver to the Navajo country who asked traders to have the Indians make lighter weight silver and to use the cut and polished stones which he had brought along. Designing, so the story goes, was also recommended in directions of heavy stamping, the use of more design elements on a single piece of jewelry, and the use of swastikas, arrows, and a few other designs not used previously by Navajos.

Stamps for impressing designs on the silver were used before and during this period and continued to be ever more important from this time onward. Earlier stamp patterns were inspired by those used on Mexican leather; after this 1899 incident, a great many new decorative themes developed, many coming from contact with the white man. This was a normal exchange of ideas between two cultures. These dies, of course, greatly facilitated decoration of silver, and offered the potential for far more variety than ever before. Usually a man cut his own dies, earlier from scrap metal, later, on the ends of files, or still later from commercial blanks.

From 1900 to 1930, tourist traffic increased greatly in the Southwest, encouraging the Navajo in his silvercrafting. During this period, the Mexican coins which had been used from 1890 were no longer available; silver slugs took their place. Slugs were about an inch and one-half square and one-eighth of an inch in thickness and weighed an ounce. These were usually available at trading posts. They continued to be used sparingly even after they were replaced by sheet silver; one trader reported that he was still using slugs in 1940. The same techniques continued to be used in this period, wrought and cast. The Navajo still made much jewelry for himself and other Indians, which included bracelets, necklaces, earrings, and buttons. Even dress ornaments such as V-shaped collar decorations and straight silver pieces plus medicine pouches were still made. Produced for the white man were all of the above pieces of jewelry plus a number of items not used by the

Indian, and including, among others, cigarette and other boxes; knife, fork, and spoon sets of various sizes and shapes; brooches; ash trays, and other small dishes. Bow guards, a silver or silver and turquoise-decorated leather wrist guard, were made primarily for the Indian, but occasionally these pieces reached the white trader and buyer. Casting of ingots for the making of wrought pieces was still practiced. Cast pieces were, of course, still made.

From 1930 to 1950 many incidents of interest occurred in the production of Navajo Indian silver. The basic trends of the 1930s continued, with some additions along the way. Toward the end of this decade, channel was developed by the Zuñis but in time came to be important to the Navajos. This technique involved the marking off of small areas of various shapes by standing thin silver strips on end. These "boxes" were then filled with a single turquoise in each. Silver and stone were leveled off by buffing. Too, turquoise became more abundant and a larger number of pieces of Navajo silver were set with this stone, a concession to the white man for most of the Indians' efforts were now for this trade.

Rodney Nelson is a smiling example of Navajo youth. Most up-to-date is he in his fine suit, collared shirt, and a bola tie in a silver version of the Navajo "wedding basket" design.

Beautiful indeed is this Navajo sleeping baby, its soft skin unequalled. Secured to its cradle board by a hand-woven sash, the child is dressed in a velveteen blouse. The inevitable touch of turquoise rests at the baby's throat.

Hoskie T. Boyd is a Navajo living at Kayenta, Arizona. The costume he is wearing is, reputedly, an original Navajo warrior's outfit which was commonly used in wars against other tribes. Made of cow or buffalo hide, the shield was their only defense. Hoskie is employed by the Bureau of Indian Affairs at the Kayenta boarding school.

Right: Old (far right) and new (center and left) Navajo belts. Butterflies in bow guard pattern are interesting in the third belt, as is the substitution of coral in the center example. The first belt is more modern in its central treatment, and in the handling of the Lone Mountain stones.

Above: In this Navajo necklace, the naja is fairly traditional and the squashes have added decoration in inner flanges and outer silver drops. Below: Plain beads still dominate Navajo necklaces, even though pendants and pieces replacing the squash blossom may be more elaborate. In the larger necklace (right), the work about the McGinnis turquoise is fairly reserved.

One bracelet form not mentioned before but long a Navajo favorite continued into this 1930-1950 period. This was made of two triangular bracelets with a twisted wire between them; flat silver platforms may or may not have straddled the three pieces at one or three places to support one or three turquoises. Plain narrow, medium, or wide bands of silver were unset or set with one, three, or many stones. Unhappily, stamping added thunderbirds, Indian heads, and other themes not used in earlier years. Rings remained rather the same as previously—a single stone or two or three large stones, or sometimes a larger central stone with small ones all around. The latter was a Zuñi style long favored by the Navajos.

During this period squash blossom necklaces continued to be made. Perhaps the chief difference was in lighter weight silver used in all the beads; however, najas were still predominantly cast pieces and therefore heavier. Many squashes were still minus turquoise settings, although all along an occasional piece might carry the stone in the crescent and, less often, in each squash bead. Some necklaces of plain round or nearly round beads began to be popular; these were without benefit of turquoise, but a few were stamped. Some squashes and plain bead necklaces were still heavy—these were often gems of craftsmanship.

Concha belts, made from the large round or oval plates of silver, changed in several ways. The older belts had six conchas, some seven; the later ones had a larger number of plates which varied according to individual sizes of conchas. Some belts were made up of as many as fifteen to twenty of these discs. Too, there was a growing popularity of turquoise settings; the earliest belts, of course, used no turquoise. When he did begin to use turquoise, the Navajo rarely set more than one stone in the center of each concha, with additional settings surrounding this central one, a rather unusual style.

World War II played an interesting role in relation to Indian jewelry. Although others were unable to get silver during the war years for ornaments, the Indian was, for many of them, particularly Zuñis, depended upon this for a livelihood. Production did subside, of course, but there was some Navajo work. After the war was over, a renewed public interest encouraged the Navajo in directions of more sophisticated styles of jewelry. Sheet silver had been available in a variety of weights for about two decades, thus enabling the Indian to do more refined work than ever before. For instance, bezels could be easily and well cut from a thin piece of sheet silver. Despite a continuation of a quantity of inferior work, much of which perpetuated "gingerbread" styles, Navajos were going back to early design executed in the finest craftsmanship.

Another interesting trend of the post-war years was participation by the Navajos in the making of channel work. Often the Navajo made the silver and the Zuñi cut and set the stones. Sometimes mosaic or inlay work was done in the same way. Two favorite subjects were the rainbow man and knifewing bird. Frequently a Zuñi smith cut the turquoise, jet, and shell and glued them to a piece of paper. Then he took them to a trader, usually in Gallup, who, in turn, gave them to a Navajo who set them in silver. This, of course, again stresses the Navajo's basic interest in silversmithing, with stone work secondary. Except for those few stones which seem to have been Navajo-cut, and crudely so, in the early days of the use of turquoise, this material has been provided for him ready cut and polished.

From the 1950s on, turquoise was used in larger quantities than ever before. The growing popularity of the blue stone among buyers encouraged the Navajo in this direction. By the 1970s, quite a lot of Navajo silver was really overwhelmed by turquoise. Many of the old forms have prevailed, but their appearance is quite different in some instances when comparing them with old styles.

Another trend in Navajo silver which started in the 1940s and continued thereafter was the use of overlay. This involves the sweating of a cut-out piece of silver onto a plain piece of the same size and shape. Started by the Hopis, this style was introduced to the Navajos by traders and others. One trader had a group of Navajos working for him at his post. Not only did he introduce the silversmiths to the new technique, but he also supplied designs for them to execute. Some of these, incidentally, came from a publication on Mimbres pottery, a prehistoric ware developed in southwestern New Mexico. The life form designs in this book were featured by the Navajo craftsmen in overlay.

Perhaps the major developments from 1950 to 1975 might be briefly summarized as follows. For about fifteen years, there was a plateau, with relatively few basic changes in the craft itself actually occurring. However, within this period a great many things happened which were to lead to actual changes in Navajo silver and turquoise. Many exhibits of Indian crafts created more interest on the part of the buying public. So too did the appearance of a number of publications. The Institute of American Indian Art was set up in Santa Fe in the early 1960s; it became a vital influence in new directions in all craft areas, including silver. New competitive shows were established. Although primarily interested in painting, the Scottsdale Show (Arizona) soon became a vital influence in bettering silver and turquoise, and a supporter of new trends.

Slight wonder, then, that the end of the 1960s and the first half of the 1970s saw some of the greatest changes in Indian crafts and particularly of silver. But few of these trends can be mentioned here. Among others, there was an interesting increase in physical size of necklaces, bracelets, rings, and some other items of Navajo make. With the terrific increase in quantity of jewelry during the first half of the 1970 decade, there was a comparable decrease in quality. Yet, at the same time, some individual craftsmen kept up very high standards of production, with some jewelry more beautiful and finer in workmanship than any ever before; also, some work was more creative than at any previous time.

Gold came into use and was beautifully handled by a few Navajos. There is less plain silver; perhaps the greatest use of turquoise reflects public demand. This terrific demand plus the high price of turquoise has brought about the reworking of old mines and the development of new ones. The result has been a greater variety of turquoise in Navajo jewelry in the first half of the 1970s than at any previous time.

Photographs of modern Navajo silver speak eloquently for trends in this craft. Turquoise is pleasingly complimented by coral, the latter often in polished branches. Coral alone finds greater favor today with the Navajos. Free form stones are used—as a cluster in a bracelet, or as a large single stone in a ring. Squash blossoms have become elaborated; one has a flower-like extension set with beautifully matched, brilliantly red coral. More stones are set with crenulated bezels. More ornate decoration appears on the silver, despite the presence of stones. Matched sets of bracelets, earrings, rings, and necklaces now are often crafted by Navajos. Conchas have become elaborated in many directions—in varied arrangements of filed, chiseled, or stamped decoration; in excessively small scallops at the edges; in turquoise placed at the rim, inside scallop points, or toward the center of the disc. The tiny butterflies between conchas may be in new shapes, such as bow guards, complete with repoussé and leaves.

Above: Lesley Francisco, a Navajo from Crystal Trading Post, Navajo, New Mexico, wears a velveteen blouse of rich red which is intensified by a turquoise chunk necklace. Very modern is the brooch at his throat.
Below: Thelma Begay, Navajo, has donned the old-style woven dress of her tribeswomen. This featured broad end panels of red with dark blue or black designs and a wide black center. The dress is caught over both shoulders. Her hair is done in the traditional "chongo" or figure-8 style. Her necklace is interesting in its naja-enclosed stones, and her brooch is of Zuñi cluster style — much favored by Thelma's tribe.

Perhaps one of the most interesting trends in Navajo jewelry has been the use of gold. Simplicity bespeaks elegance in a pair of bola tie tips, or in simple twisted rope around a large piece of Bisbee turquoise. Fancy styles so popular in all gold work today are reflected in the Navajos' use of heavy filigree, plain or fancy leaves, or tiny flowerlets. Yet another gold piece again bespeaks the Navajo's first love in metalwork—simplicity—in a handsomely crafted necklace. The plain and squash beads and the naja are silk-smooth, and, in the latter, is a last touch of elegance, a single turquoise.

Arlene Jane Yazzie is a charming little Navajo girl from the Pine Springs area. A first grader, she likes to help her mother set the table, cook, and work about the house. She already wears tribal jewelry with aplomb.

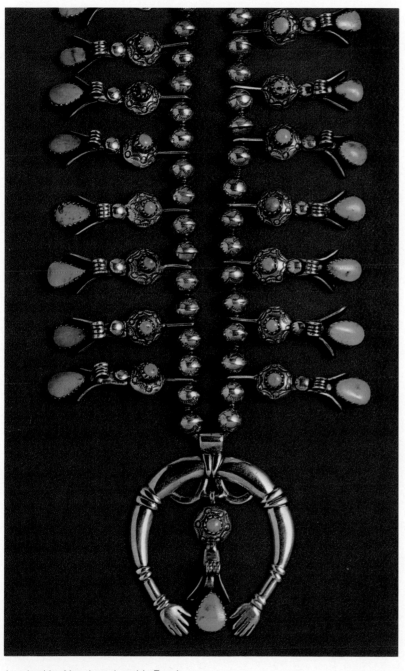

Inspired by Navajo styles, this Frank Patania-designed squash blossom necklace reflects the rich simplicity of which he was so capable. There is a pleasing balance between silver and the soft-toned Morenci turquoise (ca 1950). Crafted by Jimmie Herald, Navajo.

Left: Navajo and Zuñi rings. All of the single and two-stone pieces are Navajo except the fetish ring (below long coral example). The two cluster and two row-types are typically Zuñi, as is the coral-channel ring at the bottom. Navajo in workmanship are the two nugget styles set in old gold.

Darrine Nelson, a lad from Ft. Defiance, Arizona, typifies the full-cheeked Navajo boy. His dress is traditional in head tie and in shell bead and turquoise chunk necklace, of simple style for children.

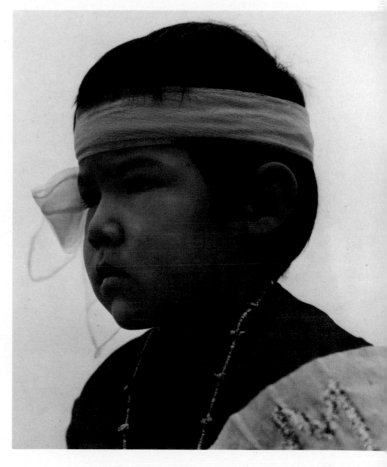

A Navajo belt and bracelet and a Santo Domingo necklace. All stones are Villa Grove except the jacla in the necklace, and it is Persian. The necklace is a style long made by this Pueblo group and worn largely by Navajos.

Bolas, again modern "Navajo style." And again, turquoise responds to new ideas — gold, leaves and flowers, and a heavily winged kachina — all very different from typical Navajo style craftsmanship. Left to right, top to bottom: Landers Blue spiderweb, Blue Gem, Lone Mountain nugget, Blue Gem, Persian, Persian, Lone Mountain spiderweb, Morenci.

Although executed by a Navajo, this turquoise and shell set of necklace, bracelet, ring, and earrings is more in the Zuñi tradition in design. Fine stones and rich shell pieces are well cut; the silver craftsmanship is clean and precise.

Fannie Toledo, Miss Eastern Navajo of Crown Point, New Mexico. Her lovely skin and beautiful eyes do indeed make her a queen. A silver and turquoise crown was crafted for her reign. Otherwise, she wears the "jacla" string-bead type of earrings and choker. Over her right shoulder is a native style hand-woven belt.

Right: Solid gold or gold on silver bracelets, all but center top called "Navajo style," but there are many changes in forms and in additions to the basic form. The chief reminder of Navajo work is in the single stone or the small number of them. Choice of turquoise is important in the use of gold; particularly pleasing here is Morenci (second row, left and center) and Persian (bottom, left and center). Left to right, top to bottom: coral, Persian, Lone Mountain, Morenci, Morenci, Lone Mountain, Persian, Persian, Persian, Persian, Persian, Burnham.

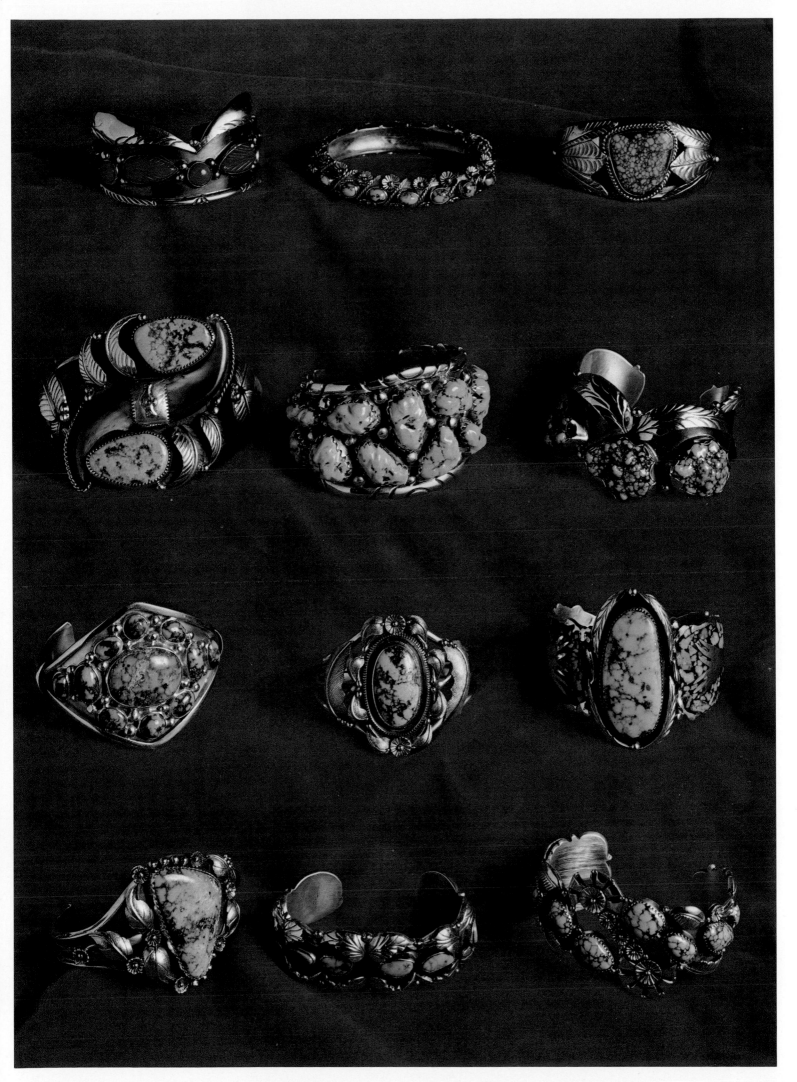

The necklace on the right is more Navajo in its simplicity than the other two. However, embellishment is typical of some pieces today, as exhibited in the Navajo necklace to the left. Above is a Taos-made piece; it is Navajo in style only in the simple silver squash blossoms proper and in the use of a few larger stones, here Blue Gem; the "furbelows" are not Navajo.

The same dominant simplicity of the best Navajo silver is featured in this gold squash blossom necklace, executed by a Zapotec Indian. Slightly more decorative is the Santo Domingo bracelet, and decidedly ornate is the upper ring.

Above: Burnished silver overlay and the use of amethyst, garnets, lapis, ivory, ebony, ironwood and Kingman spiderweb turquoise make this group of bracelets unique. Although there is a Hopi resemblance, both groupings were designed and made by non-Indians. Below: High grade blue gem is set into 14kt gold in the bear claw bola. Landers Blue turquoise was used in the second bola, the gold squash blossom necklace and the single-stoned ring. Diamonds were added to the ring featuring three Persian stones.

Beautiful White House Ruins, Canyon de Chelly. The ruins are so named because of the white-washed wall of the upper rooms; they stand out most vividly against the red sandstone cliffs of the canyon. Many such prehistoric sites are found in this canyon of northeastern Arizona.

Variety of bracelets, and all Navajo made except the Lone Mountain spiderweb piece (lower left) which is Zuñi made. Newer developments in Navajo work are illustrated in the "gingerbread" around the Landers turquoise (center bottom) and the use of coral. Left to right, top to bottom: Bisbee, coral, Lone Mountain spiderweb, Lone Mountain spiderweb, Number 8 spiderweb, Lone Mountain spiderweb, Landers Blue spiderweb and coral, Bisbee, Lone Mountain spiderweb, Lone Mountain spiderweb, Landers Blue spiderweb, Lone Mountain spiderweb.

Much more elaborate than the usual Navajo work are this necklace
and the belt. More stones in the former overpower the squash
blossoms; multiple radiate lines and scallops about the bezels differ from
the massive simplicity which has always been featured by the
Navajo silversmith.

Jim Abeita, one of the fine young Navajo easel artists of today, is from Crown Point, New Mexico. He has won many awards for his paintings. Here he adheres to Navajo tradition in hat with decorative band, in jacla necklace, bracelets and ring.

Styled in comparable manner are all of these gold-on-silver and turquoise brooches. Leaves ornament their edges, while flowerlets are inserted in the left and right center pieces, and a bit of coral branch in the latter. Left to right, top to bottom: Kingman, Persian, Morenci, Morenci, Persian, Burnham, Persian, Persian.

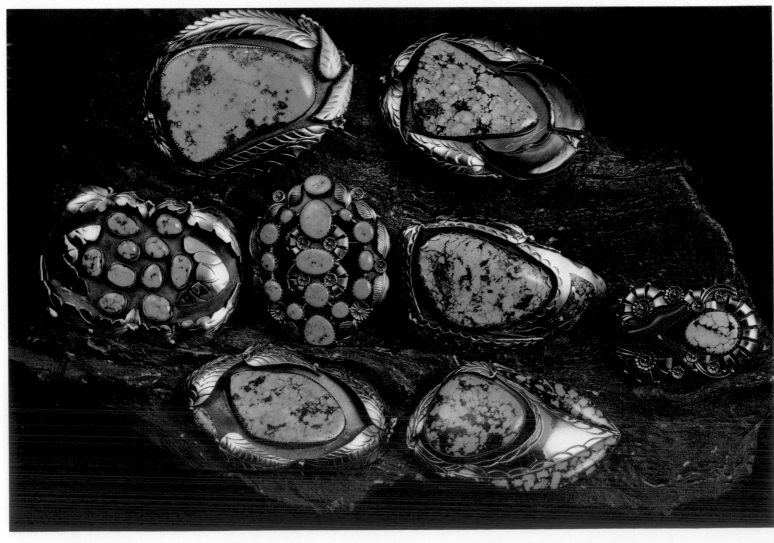

Navajo made are a bola slide, bracelet, ring, earrings and necklace, all featuring a common theme — a kachina. Lone Mountain turquoise emphasizes kilt, eyes and headgear of the figure.

The Zuñi-made necklaces to the right and left reflect the versatility of turquoise as it is most attractive in both the delicate and elaborate metal work in one and in the simple gold work of the other. The Hopi necklace and bracelet in the center contrast with both of the Zuñi pieces in their severe simplicity of design and crafting. These pieces illustrate some of the contrasts between Puebloan and Navajo styles.

Silver and coral, Navajo crafted necklaces. The lower piece is mindful of an
earlier Navajo style but is somewhat elaborated in the extension of silver to
hold the coral in front of the squash blossom. Too, the tiny flower added
to the naja or pendant and to the second necklace is a further fancier detail.

A variety of Navajo and Zuñi crafts pieces. Distinctly Navajo in workmanship or style are the two muddlers (bottom), the tiny canteen just above them, and the shell-shaped pill box (right). Typically Zuñi is the fetish necklace, and the box above it combines Navajo metal work and Zuñi inlay. The rest of the pieces could be by craftsmen of either group; the two gold bracelets, hair piece, and two crosses are Navajo.

Typical Navajo salad set, necklaces partially in box, and boxes. The third necklace and pendant are Hopi, crafted by Preston Monongye. Typical of earlier Navajo work is the simplicity and stamping of the silver and the use of single stones.

Fine, clean lines characterize much Navajo jewelry, early and late. Limited use of turquoise is another Navajo trait in silversmithing. Here they are elegantly combined, particularly in the belt on the left.

On this Navajo necklace is a massive single Kingman natural stone which is surrounded by a bezel and several additional decorative devices, a typical modern trend. Balanced horns (or claws) at the two sides are offset by a single sharp claw pendant from the main part of the necklace; the break in symmetry in the stone is another modern element of style.

W. Dean Wilson was Judge of the Courts of the Navajo tribe from 1960 to 1975. During World War II, he served as a Navajo Code Talker in the U.S. Marine Corps; the Indian Code was never broken by the enemy. Wilson belongs to a tribal dance and song troupe. Currently, he writes a weekly news item, "Pow Wow News," for Navajo Times. Wilson lives at Window Rock, Arizona, the tribal center.

Three Navajo belts. The top example is cast; the central one shows a modern trend in the center cluster, and the base of the bottom example is quite typical of the Navajo but has an added Zuñi inlay.

49

Right: Called "Navajo style" by some, these modern claw necklaces present a recent innovation. New ideas take over almost completely — in gold, in design — leaving but a simple bead shape in the top and central necklaces, and turquoise in all three, mindful of earlier Navajo style. Top necklace, Persian; center, Lone Mountain; lower, Burnham; and bracelet, Blue Gem.

Fine Persian turquoise is set in an unusual way in this squash blossom necklace. The beads are handmade. An Indian trader will often save a fine or unusual piece for himself.

More leaves, now used in place of the lower part of the chain (lower left), or to embrace the turquoise (upper left). All claws here are labeled "bear." Persian turquoise enhances the very un-Indian necklace at the lower right. A pleasing design involving a bird, Morenci turquoise and claws appears on the central pendant. Turquoise left to right and top to bottom: Burnham, Landers Blue, Morenci, Lone Mountain, Persian, Persian.

Dora Aweyy, of Zuñi Pueblo, wears the sweet smile of many of the elderly among Indians. Here she demonstrates a situation common to the Gallup Intertribal Ceremonials for many years. The women wear the traditional style dark dress belted at the waist with a wide red belt and a floral blouse, with a silk scarf at the neck and falling over the shoulders. Her necklace and brooches are massive and spectacular. On her head she carries a fine old style Zuñi pottery vessel.

Right: It is quite likely that Zuñis wear more jewelry than any other tribe. These performers at the Flagstaff Pow Wow are always eye-dazzling attractions.

ZUÑI

Zuñi Indian jewelry is the most delicate of all made in the Southwest today. This statement applies to much of their craft, but not to all. The time factor has a great deal to do with these matters, for in the broad picture, Zuñis started out making large pieces with sizeable stones and, through the years, worked toward ever smaller decorative stone pieces. Too, it can be said in general that the Zuñi, for the most part, was more interested in stones than metal. In fact, frequently he is referred to as a lapidary, a stone cutter, rather than a silversmith. This, too, is a relative matter, for much attractive metal crafting has been done by Zuñi Indians.

Beginning phases of metal crafting in this tribe are the same as those indicated for the Navajos—they are deeply rooted in the working of copper, brass, and iron. Probably no later than 1830-40, Mexicans were giving Zuñis pots and pans of the first two metals; from these, the Zuñis were making crosses, bracelets, rings, and a few other items of personal adornment. These pieces were worn not only by the Mexicans but also by the Zuñi tribesmen. Apparently Mexicans thought highly of these Indian metal craftsmen for often they paid a smith one sheep for a piece of his jewelry.

Work in iron seems to have taken a slightly different direction as plied by the Zuñi for he made or mended hoes and axes rather than making bridles as did the Navajo. Perhaps this was in part because the metal work other than silver was learned directly from Mexicans; however, it was also applied to the Zuñi way of life which was quite different from that of the Navajo. Sitgreaves, in his *Report of an Expedition Down the Zuñi and Colorado Rivers, 1853,* pictures a Zuñi blacksmith shop.

It was a Navajo, Atsidi Chon, who taught the first Zuñi, Lanyade, to do silver crafting. Perhaps this is why the earliest work in this metal was more like that of the Navajo in its beginning years. Little silver jewelry had been traded into Zuñi before this date, 1872, when Atsidi Chon came to live with his Zuñi friend. As to be expected, the Navajo made bridles and conchas which were new items of silver to the Zuñi. Atsidi Chon also copied the Zuñi brass cross styles in silver.

Incidentally, the type of cross first worn by the Zuñis was, reputedly, the double-armed style. Some members of this tribe had been Christianized and were required to wear the cross as a symbol of their acceptance of the new faith. Fortunately, the type of cross introduced by the conquerors was comparable to a native religious design, the highly conventionalized double-winged, elongate-bodied dragon fly. As a consequence, Zuñis wore the cross, perhaps in their hearts feeling closer to the old faith than to the new one.

Like the Navajos, the first Zuñi smiths filed designs onto their brass and copper jewelry. But Atsidi Chon brought dies, teaching his Zuñi student not only the new craft but how to make dies as well.

In early years Zuñis used the same materials as well as making the same objects as did the Navajos. American and Mexican coins were both used. Early work had no settings, and the silver style was massive. Early forms included bridles, conchas with holes in the center for lacing onto a leather base (old style) or without this hole, buttons, triangular bracelets, bow guards, plain beads, and several early types of earrings including a large hoop with a bead at the bottom. Slight wonder that it is impossible to tell early Zuñi silver from that of the early Navajo smith— they *are* one and the same!

Later Zuñi silver work has a distinctive Mexican flavor. This is probably because they were in frequent contact with several eastern puebloan people who, in turn, lived closer to Mexicans; the latter influenced the eastern villagers' silver, and this influenced the Zuñi work. Further, through trade with Mexicans there were also some direct influences on the Zuñis' work. However, it was not until they acquired better tools during later years that the Zuñis were able to craft jewelry in Mexican styles. Too, along with this influence is the use of turquoise, and this stone was apparently not used until about 1890; this helps date the Mexican style of work. Although rococo, much of this jewelry was charming. For example, in earrings it involved long or short pendants of silver, often in several rows; or several tiny squash blossoms hanging at the bottom of an earring (and it took great skill and experience to craft these); or much wire loop work, outside a stone or surrounding an elongate repoussé-design, or inside a circle; the use of many tiny drops of silver; and many combinations of these and other designs—and all dangling!

So, with the acquisition of turquoise came a great promise for new ventures in Zuñi jewelry As Zuñis continued to trade with Navajos, or to be friendly with them, quite naturally the earliest work in this stone resembled the Navajo style—a few large stones in heavy silver work. Turquoise remained scarce at Zuñi until the turn of the century when white man began to work mines in the Southwest. This scarcity also influenced size, as did quality. Large beautiful stones were hard, too hard to encourage the tedious task of cutting smaller ones from such pieces. The smaller stone was the left-over after cutting out the larger one—until the arrival of many new tools, among others, the lapidary stick, sealing wax, and the emery wheel. Then, for sure, did Zuñi lapidaries move in new directions, or perhaps one should say, revive old directions. The qualities and character of old styles of mosaic had also continued to live in other decorative work, in the small unit designs on masks, or in body painting, or in other artistic expressions.

Thus, between new tools, old traditions, and more turquoise, Zuñis began to feature the use of more and smaller stones in a single piece of jewelry. This was a gradual process; there are many pieces with stones intermediate in size between the first large ones and contemporary small ones.

The earlier plain button worn on Zuñi men's leggings and moccasins became larger brooches set with many medium or small turquoises, now to enrich the dark dresses worn by the women. Plain silver hoop earrings formerly worn by men and women alike in 1910 were also set with many turquoises and ornamented with wire filigree and dangles, to become the woman's most important item of jewelry. Many of these earrings were beautiful in design and exquisitely delicate. Men substituted a single turquoise of irregular shape for the earlier silver pieces for their ear ornaments. One piece which changed little if any was the manta pin. This was a large oval or rectangular piece of silver, running the gamut from quite plain to elaborately decorated, with stamping and repoussé.

By 1910, much Zuñi jewelry was set with an abundance of turquoise on now-popular pieces such as bracelets, bow guards, rings, squash blossom necklaces, buckles, and concha belts. One exception was the belt, for sometimes each concha had but a single central stone; however, in other instances there might be a circle of stones around this central one, usually closer to the edge.

Commercialization, so important from 1900 on among the Navajos, played no part in these earlier changes among the Zuñis. In fact, all their jewelry was made for themselves or for other Indians. This situation did not change for the Zuñis until about 1920. Prior to this date silvercrafting was of little significance economically, and that to less than ten smiths. After this date there was a growing number of smiths and by 1940, there were close to a 100. As a result, a terrific economic change occurred at Zuñi. Commercialization really became the strongest factor in change in Zuñi jewelry from this time on.

Through the years, the Zuñi smith acquired more and more equipment. This, undoubtedly, allowed for smaller and smaller stone cutting. Too, this situation may also explain the fact that some of these Zuñi craftsmen were able to and did practice a wide variety of techniques—casting, hammering, stamping, large and small stone work, with the latter in mosaic or in individual stone settings. Small stones were cut in various shapes — round, square, rectangular, oval, tear-drop, and needlepoint. The last involves cutting a long, slender stone to a point at each end. Often this is one of the most delicate pieces of Zuñi lapidary.

For some years individual small stone work was centered in straight row or cluster arrangements of turquoise, particularly in bracelets, brooches, and rings. In row work, the small stones were shaped as squares, rectangles, round forms, and diamonds, rarely in others. More limited were the stone shapes in clusters, with emphasis on round or oval forms. Typically, bracelet rows were single, double, or multiple, sometimes with as many as ten or twelve rows, an elaboration which took place later. Quite naturally the clusters were more limited in number of rows, with one or two circles of the blue stone earlier; three, four, or five later. Between stones in both styles were placed either small round balls or drops of silver, with sizes of these adjusted to the size of the stones. Often the clusters on brooches have alternate rows of oval and round stones. Too, needlepoint may be substituted for stones of other shapes in both row and cluster styles. Another and later variation was to put a row of silver work, such as repeated small bossed crescents, between the blue stones; often this gave a more sophisticated feeling to the finished brooch.

Mosaic was, of course, an ancient craft among the Zuñis. In fact, a rich tradition in turquoise, shell, and jet was inherited by this tribe from their prehistoric ancestors. However, they had been unable to get some of these materials, thus had not perpetuated this tradition except haphazardly. When silver came to them, at first they merely contained the mosaic in a metal band, on a metal base. In time, the silver came to be more significantly a part of the mosaic. It was not until about 1935 that a renewed interest came about; it was at this time that Zuñis really began serious production of mosaic. Often it was called inlay, and its merits were many. As in the traditional work, again they used a basic combination including turquoise, coral (or red stone or red shell) jet, and white shell. These symbolized the four colors of the four directions—turquoise, red, black, and white. To be sure, jewelry using these colors was not symbolic, but, perhaps, in the hearts of the smiths who made the lovely pieces featuring these shades was a peace and harmony in their creation because of this native significance.

Much outstanding craftsmanship was involved in many of these mosaics. So perfectly cut was each piece that it fitted its neighbors with hardly any evidence that they were cut separately. As mosaic became more and more popular, materials became more varied and subject matter expanded. A variety of colored shells appeared, to supplement and stress small details of representational subjects, for example, subtle shades of grays, browns, soft pinks or sharp reds, and orange. Tortoise shell was introduced, to add depth, richness, and variety of color, as was serpentine in its range of tones from pale yellow through intermediate shades to a dark green.

Through the 1960s and into the 1970s subject matter in mosaic had become so expanded that it would seem to be quite unrelated to the original threesome—the sun, knife-wing god, and rainbow man. These mythological subjects, however, never lost their favored spot, and, along with the others, reflected all of the new materials, new touches of craftsmanship—even new gaudiness which developed through the years. In numerous combinations of these materials, in many sizes and poses, were added more life subjects, among others, gods without number, including shalako and all his major attendants, or masks of the same, and, too, the spirits of other tribes, such as the Apache gans dancers; unmasked performers such as hoop dancers; full figures or heads of animals, for example, mountain sheep, bears, horses, or cattle; butteflies; frogs; and birds, including quail, roadrunners, owls, and cardinals. To be sure, the geometric was not ignored in mosaic. Varied were the forms, with a single piece combining one, two, or more elements such as rectangles, diamonds or triangles, crescents, ovoid forms, bands.

Beautifully matched No. 8 turquoise was crafted into this Zuñi necklace-belt set. Teardrop-shaped stones are featured in both pieces, but round ones were substituted for the very tiny settings in the necklace squashes.

The Zuñi lapidary was justly proud of his perfectly-cut pieces for inlay work.
Each concha of the left belt has a different subject or a different pose. The
usual perfect stone cutting and matching is very much in evidence in the
Persian stone conchas of the cluster belt. The brooch and earrings are made
14 karat gold with Lone Mountain turquoise.

Daniel Martinez of Zuñi, New Mexico, is undoubtedly a jovial fellow. His belt is more Navajo in its simplicity and limited turquoise. But his necklace is Santo Domingo style — a fine, very heavy chunk type. He also wears two large coin brooches surrounded by typical Zuñi rosette-turquoise workmanship.

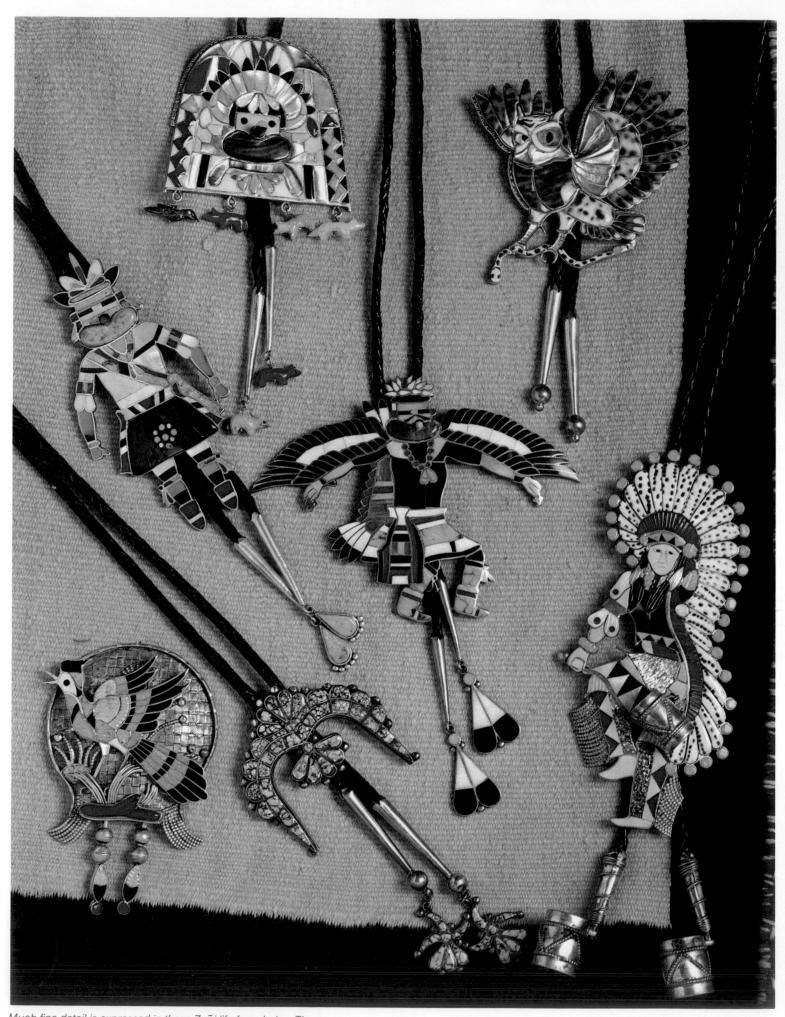

Much fine detail is expressed in these Zuñi life-form bolas. The
central eagle dancer has multiple feathers on his arms, feathers
repeated on the bola tips, plus decorative detail on kilt, sash and
turquoise moccasins.

Zuñi small stone work in two bracelets, a pair of earrings, and a necklace. Beautifully matched Morenci turquoise enhances the bracelet and earrings which were made to go with the necklace, while the old pawn cluster brooch in the center is set with both teardrop and round Lone Mountain turquoise.

One other aspect regarding mosaic is the terrific elaboration within this style in two ways—one, as it is used alone, and two, as it is combined with one or more other stone techniques, such as channel. Perhaps its greatest merit as used alone has been its refinement in recent years, utilizing smaller and a greater variety of stones and shell in a single piece. Sometimes the individual stones or pieces of shell are very tiny, for example, when used for the eye in a dancer's or animal's face.

Channel is usually referred to as a Zuñi style, perhaps because this tribe was the first of the Southwest Indians to express the technique; 1940 is the approximate date for channel beginnings. It is quite likely that there was much borrowing from small stone work at first, later from inlay, in the newer technique. Channel is the making of cells or a honeycomb-like arrangement by soldering onto a silver base very thin upright pieces of silver. Into each cell or space so created is placed a flat-surfaced stone. Silver and stone are buffed off to a common smoothness. At first turquoise only was used; quickly shell and coral were added, each used alone in a single piece of jewelry. In time numerous combinations of materials appeared in channel, and tops of stones were often left rounded.

Earlier channel was crafted in geometric designs, but in time fine Zuñi work of this type concentrated on life forms. Perhaps some of the finest and most delicate work ever expressed by Southwet Indians has been in a combination of inlay and channel to produce life themes, or, even, simple compositions.

Angular geometric channel styles included everything from a simple row of rectangles to a composite of steps, triangles, and diamonds. The simplicity of turquoise alone gave way to the use of jet, coral, and turquoise in a single piece of geometric style. Also, the earlier angular geometric was quickly joined by curvilinear designs. By the 1950s life forms were finding favor as crafted in channel, particularly birds. However, all other creatures which had been subject matter for jewelry were done in channel sooner or later. This trend also meant the use of various materials; therefore, several colors in combination in a single piece of channel jewelry was a style favored to the mid-1970s.

Navajo influence persists through the years, and slight wonder—Zuñis bought dies from Navajos, members of the latter tribe frequently visited or lived on the Zuñi Reservation, trade between the two tribes continued through the years, Navajos admired and wore a lot of Zuñi jewelry, and traders were constantly having a Zuñi lapidary and a Navajo smith cooperate in the production of a single piece of jewelry.

Some of this Navajo influence is to be noted in such details as cabachon settings which are smooth and rounded, oval or hemispherical stones, often large in size. Although more popular among the Navajos, they were, nonetheless, produced early and late among the Zuñis. Also, around the 1950s, the Zuñis began to use nuggets in their silver crafting; these contrasted sharply with the cabochons in their free forms with all of the natural irregularities left on

the surface of each piece. Nuggets were sometimes used in channel, but they were at their best in larger sizes and either individually set or combined with limited additional material, such as a stem or twig of coral. Some pieces of this kind were handsome. On occasion, the design of the entire brooch, or whatever the piece of jewelry might be, would follow the outline of the irregular turquoise nugget and coral pieces.

Other areas of contact between the Navajos and Zuñis include the bezel or setting for stones plus additional decorative silver work. Quite generally, the Navajo used a plain, even-edged housing while the Zuñis' was scalloped or pointed. The latter has always been patiently cut by the Zuñis and often it is beautifully done; in small stone work it

Unusual is the hinged Zuñi bracelet set with Villa Grove turquoise and branch coral. Unusual, too, is the shape of the second bracelet set with free-form turquoise and branch coral. Distinctly Zuñi in design but crafted by a Navajo is the inlay belt ringed by coral.

Babela, an 85-year-old Zuñi, reflects some physical features of the American Indian, particularly high cheek bones. Conventional dress of his tribe is to be noted in his dark shirt, a beautiful, contrasting turquoise chunk and shell bead necklace, large bird pin and elaborate head tie.

Clara Pincion, Zuñi Pueblo, a woman between 97 and 103 years old, certainly has worn her years well. Her dress and jewelry reflect typical Puebloan styles. Over her floral blouse is a silk scarf; about her neck is a multiple strand of coral beads and chunk turquoise.

is often most delicately cut. It may be added that Navajos sometimes cut their bezels with fancy edges, and, by the same token, Zuñis may leave theirs plain on occasion. With very large stones it has sometimes been necessary to add finger-like prongs to hold the turquoise in place.

In the making of the silver itself, it is not easy to determine who influenced whom. Let it be said, rather, that the following traits are to be found in the work of craftsmen of both tribes. In recent years there has been more elaboration in the direction of increased bead size. Sometimes they may be graduated from small to large, particularly where the entire design tends to be free form. The larger sizes of beads have also invited additional work on them, such as stamping; stamping also is added to prongs and various devices used as fillers between stones. One of the interesting treatments of prongs is to stamp them so that they resemble shells.

Zuñis, like other Southwest Indians, have done some crafting in gold. Here, as in other late work, there is quite a bit of the metal showing, much of it of elaborate workmanship. In one squash blossom necklace more plain gold shows, indicating that Zuñis can and sometimes do craft in a simple and elegant manner. In another necklace, the squashes are simply crafted, with exquisitely delicate needlepoint setting off the gold to perfection.

Other elaborations occur in the production of jewelry of the mid-1970s, as illustrated in the following examples. Bolas are more ornate than ever before. Figures of gans dancers are enclosed by wide borders of filed silver plates. Sets of shalako performers are presented in dance postures and in exquisite detail in facial features and in costume detail—to the pleating on a dress cuff! Bracelets

(Text continued on page 67)

Della Appa, Zuñi Pueblo, reputedly was the first Zuñi woman silversmith. Typical of all Zuñi women are the bobbed hair, fine turquoise drop earrings, heavily turquoise-encrusted necklace, and a large, flashy brooch. Characteristic, too, is the silk scarf about her shoulders.

Obviously Zuñi are the three mask buckles, crafted in channel and inlay; so too is the cluster piece made of irregularly shaped Kingman turquoise (center top). The three single-stone buckles and the one with two stones are typically Navajo in style. Called "Navajo style Zuñi made" is the buckle ornamented with a snake. Turquoise center and bottom rows, left to right: Persian, Fox, Blue Gem, Burnham, Bisbee.

A beautiful example of Zuñi cluster work, particularly in the fine twisted
wire and drops between and around rows or other units of stones. Well-
matched are the No. 8 turquoise stones in their rich, intense blue coloring.

Rather more formal designing is exhibited in this Zuñi necklace and in the left bracelet, executed in channel. More traditional in subject matter and execution are the three central bracelets done in mosaic and inlay.

Zuñi Indians make the finest fetish necklaces. Materials run the gamut from turquoise to shell, coral, mother-of-pearl, serpentine, abalone, to ivory. Subjects include bears and birds, with occasional others. Workmanship varies from crude to very refined. The above is of excellent quality.

Award-winning seven-strand Zuñi fetish necklace.

Wilbert Tucson, Zuñi, New Mexico, is the son of a famous jewelry craftsman. His blue-black hair is typical of Indians. He wears parts of ceremonial paraphernalia plus Zuñi style jewelry, a coral and turquoise necklace and a coin and turquoise brooch.

Leo Quftawki, once a governor of his Pueblo, Zuñi, New Mexico, is dressed in festive attire, with a bright flowered shirt, headband, a heavy chunk turquoise necklace, and large turquoise earrings. A native woven belt is thrust over his right shoulder to the left side of his waist.

are filled with overly long, beautifully cut needlepoint, each row completed with traditional silver wire and drops, or with four rows of small rectangular stones complemented with tiny silver balls between rows. A bowguard combines a mass of silver which enfolds a large free form turquoise with other stones and a wandering snake form. Large rings depict masks in a variety of stones. Coral enjoys great favor in many pieces — alone, in combination with one other material, or with several materials.

Some of the most exquisite pieces are brooches or pendants decorated with small scenes worked out in a combination of inlay and channel, such as birds on branches complete with flowers or munching on cherries. Necklaces and belts are wondrous in their elaborate overlay-inlay or inlay-channel crafting. Motifs in these are as varied as materials—they run the gamut from elaborate geometrics to kachinas, masks—or just ornate turquoise or coral cabochon or nugget arrangements. And weaving in and out throughout all the subjects are the ubiquitous sun, rainbow god, and knifewing!

Above: Dewey Haskie, another "old timer" from the Pueblo of Zuñi, New Mexico. Quiet peace is registered in the lines of his mouth and eye wrinkles. His chunk style necklace is a fine piece of work. Hair tie is traditional. Below: Mrs. Law Tesyatugtetas wears a heavily encrusted squash blossom and a spectacular brooch. She has little record of her age but knows she is over 95.

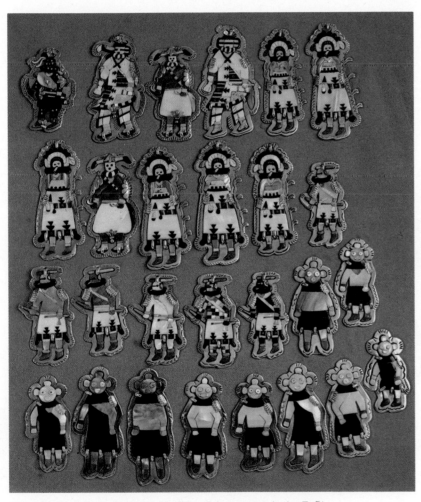

An amazing array of figures, including all that appear in the Zuñi Shalako dance. This includes the six Shalako (four in the second row, two in the first), mudheads (eight in the bottom row, two in the row above), Big Ear (top row) and others. Using a variety of materials, the costumes and masks are quite realistically portrayed.

Left: A medley of forms, materials and techniques are combined in these Zuñi pins. Traditional is the teardrop and round stone brooch (left center). Detail is fine in all the creatures, from the tiny inlay hummingbird (top left) to the coral, jet and shell channel and mosaic butterfly (bottom left).

The watch band is in Zuñi style but is Navajo made. The other three bracelets are Zuñi made: left is a row bracelet made "different" by substitution of coral and shell in place of all-turquoise; a unique piece (top right) in the diagonal placement of turquoise; and a rather ornate version of the Zuñi style inlay bird-on-branch.

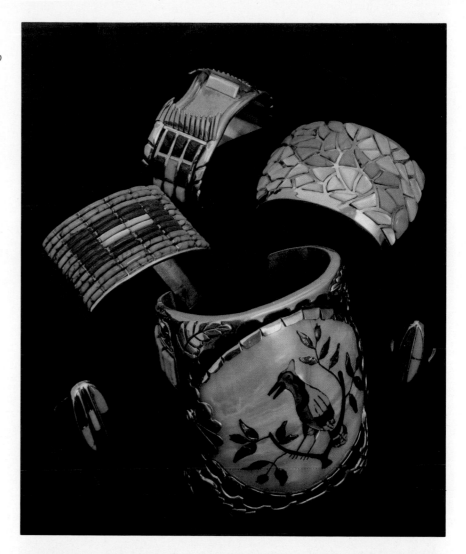

Traditional in concept and craftsmanship are these Zuñi pieces: in the squash blossom, a massive stone cluster which overpowers the small blossom and the double-band naja; a bent cluster bracelet with a row of crescents to relieve the heavy turquoise work; and an oval brooch with teardrop stones to match those in the other pieces.

Left: Zuñi belt, bola and ring, all decorated with an active Apache Gans dancer with costume and headgear rather realistically portrayed in turquoise, jet, serpentine and shell.

Left: A sampling of classic Zuñi bracelets. Fine craftsman-ship is illustrated in the rosette needlepoint (center right), as is true of the tiny square and rectangular multi-row styles, of Morenci turquoise (left, lower and upper). The remaining three cluster styles effectively utilize different types of turquoise: Lone Mountain spiderweb (top), Bisbee (center left) and Number 8 (lower right).

Morenci turquoise is perfectly cut for the Zuñi needlepoint necklace and earrings to the left while the second necklace displays a fine quality Blue Gem stone.

Rather unusual is this abundance of settings in Hopi overlay silver. The pendant effectively combines an age-old tribal bird theme with coral. Masks in overlay are cleverly combined with turquoise in the bracelet (to the right) and the bola tie, as is the double bear paw motif on the buckle (upper left). Crafted by Phillip Sekaquaptewa.

HOPI

The story of Hopi jewelry making parallels that of other Southwestern pueblos in that it was a late development. For some years they had been acquiring a few pieces of silver from the Navajos, and, also, had been experimenting in the making of a few odds and ends from scraps of copper and brass. The Zuñi, Lanyade, is credited with teaching silver work to Sikyatali, the first Hopi to learn this new craft. Adair says this was about 1898, while Colton reports that it was between 1890 and 1895. Regardless of the date, the first Hopi learned a style that was definitely Navajo, for the Zuñis perpetuated this type of workmanship throughout the 1890s.

In the usual sequence of events, Sikyatali taught other Hopis. By 1906, there were several smiths on each of the three Hopi mesas. There were occasional expressions of originality among these Hopi smiths, yet Navajo techniques and styles of silver work dominated their production for some thirty to forty years.

Not a great deal of jewelry was crafted by these early smiths, for the Hopis were still able to trade with their Navajo neighbors for what they desired. Some believe that they concentrated on the making of small pieces, such as rings, bracelets, and buttons; however, the fact is that they did make some belts, necklaces, and bow guards. The horse was not as important to the Hopis as it was to the Navajos, therefore they did not make bridle and saddle decorations in these early years. As noted, there were strong Navajo influences, but occasional pieces reflected a distinctly Hopi flavor in design.

Limited production of silver on the part of Hopis might well be explained in economic factors, for they played a significant part. Until after World War II, the craftsmen of this tribe were unable to meet the needs of their own people; certainly they did not produce anything for the competitive field of the white man. This can be attributed to several factors: one was that there were no traders backing the smiths by supplying both materials and a market as was true of Zuñis and Navajos. It is reported that as late as 1940 many of these Hopi puebloans were still wearing a large quantity of Zuñi and Navajo jewelry —which would further indicate that there was limited production.

During these early years the Hopis made both hammered and cast pieces of jewelry, favoring the former. Bow guards were sometimes cast in Navajo designs, concha belts were distinctly Navajo in style. Many other pieces of Hopi silver reflected such specific Navajo influences as form, decoration with silver drops, heavy silver set with a few large stones, stamped designs on many pieces, and plain bezels encasing fairly large turquoises. During one period of leaner years, one Hopi used copper and brass for his jewelry because silver was scarce; too, he set some bracelets with bits of colored glass "for turquoise was too scarce to use." Another Hopi made a practice of producing earrings of mosaic on a wooden base, this a matter of calling on Hopi tradition and style for inspiration. To be sure, other pieces had a distinct Hopi feeling of design, or at least leaned in this direction. Too, occasional Zuñi influences appeared, such as the dragonfly design.

Then, in the 1930s, the Museum of Northern Arizona, Flagstaff, tried to influence the Hopis in the direction of creating designs in silver along their own traditional lines. Little or no success was achieved. However, it is possible that a seed was planted, for immediately following World War II the Hopis moved in these directions. Briefly, they established an on-the-job training program, with government support. A quonset hut was set up at New Oraibi. Fred Kabotie, a Hopi painter, was designer for the group, and a Hopi smith of many years' experience, Paul Saufki, taught the craft to the veterans who were enrolled. Two eighteen-month classes were put through this training program. Some of the men continued to follow silversmithing either on a part-time or full-time basis; others dropped by the wayside. Designing featured Hopi sources; they were inspired by basketry, pottery, and textiles. However, other sources, such as prehistoric Mimbres pottery, were also explored.

A substantial base was established through this training program, both in terms of quality of jewelry and in design. Many of these trainees produced jewelry for the Hopi Arts and Crafts Guild, as did other craftsmen. The Guild built a shop and working quarters on Second Mesa in 1961. This center continues to be important in Hopi silversmithing.

For years very little or no turquoise was used in guild work; this situation changed in the 1970s with the appearance of more of the blue stone settings. Rarely are other materials such as coral or shell employed in any Hopi work. Large forms were also scarce, for the Guild centered on small items such as brooches, pendants, buckles, cuff links, rings, earrings, bracelets, tie tacks, tie bars, hair pieces, and necklaces. More commonly the latter are small chokers, although some squash blossom types were made featuring overlay pieces in place of the blossoms. Choker necklaces began to appear in the fifties, and remained popular through the sixties and into the seventies; their delicacy is a distinct attribute.

The Guild has encouraged its producers to continue with native design, although some time after its founding, their workers have tapped other sources, such as prehistoric Hohokam and Anasazi pottery motifs and pictographs. Most of the silver designing which can be identified as Hopi has been and is highly stylized, much is asymmetrical; however, an occasional realistic theme appears, such as a kachina dancer.

As to Hopi technology, it is significant to refer to those methods of working silver required in the specifications of the Museum of Northern Arizona during the 1930s' effort to develop a tribal style. Designs presented by this group required not only the usual methods of forming a piece, plus filing and stamping for decoration, but also overlay, applique, and cut-out. Undoubtedly these early recommendations affected later work. Overlay involved the preparation of two pieces of silver, identical in size and shape. On one is inscribed the desired design, usually from a template; this is then cut out with a jeweler's saw. The piece with the cut out area is sweated and soldered onto the plain piece; next the lower part is treated so as to blacken it. The usual smoothing of edges and polishing

Rather typical pieces made by the Hopis in overlay, a buckle (top left), a pair of earrings (top center), mudhead decorated pendant on handmade chain (top right), a key ring ornamented with a bear paw (lower right), belt buckle (center right), left-handed kachina pin (center), and a brooch with the mask of Big Ear.

Ira Tewawina, a Hopi from Second Mesa, Arizona, reflects the strong character and firmness of many of his tribe's people. Tradition lingers in his headband, his shell-bead turquoise chunk and coral necklaces, and the bandolier across his chest.

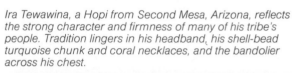

Hopi overlay expresses a sophisticated theme on the elongate necklace pieces and earrings, and adds a lighter touch in the spread-wing man-bird pendant and bracelet.

follows, leaving the lower black design in contrast to the higher polished areas. This overlay is a distinctive Hopi style, despite the fact that it is also expressed by Navajos and Zuñis. If a smith is expert in the cutting process, he can then sweat the section which has been removed to another plain piece, thus producing a design in bas relief, or one form of appliqué. Cut-out is, as the name implies, a cutting through the one thickness of silver to outline the design or to leave an open area within it. It has been used for some time for design creation, but has never been as popular as overlay.

Early in the 1960s, three Hopi brothers, the Sekaquaptewas, established an independent shop, Hopicrafts, first in Phoenix, later at New Oraibi. Peter Shelton, Jr. was their designer. Workmanship on jewelry was greatly superior, and a beautiful finish was attained by simply rubbing each piece with steel wool, this giving a lovely soft and satiny finish. Too, they used an interesting texturing of the lower black areas of overlay. Hopicrafts also stressed originality in designs. All in all, this private enterprise has been most influential in raising the quality of Hopi silver crafting.

One of the most famous of Hopis is the incredible metal craftsman, Charles Loloma. He left his Reservation for advanced education and teaching but, as all Hopis do, returned and established his studio close to his natal village of Hotevilla. The broad features of his tribe are reflected in his face.

In addition to Paul Saufkie, several other Hopi smiths have become famous for their unusual craftsmanship, among them Charles Loloma and Preston Monongye. At first Loloma practiced casting only, later he added other techniques; also he used gold as well as silver. His combinations of methods and materials are outstanding; these, plus originality of design, elevate his work to recognition on an international level. Loloma has combined silver and gold, he has effectively utilized ivory and turquoise, and other stones in exotic patterning. He has created a design on a bracelet in multi-colored relief patterns, with the inside of the same piece lined with lovely mosaic. Irregularities in sizes and shapes of decorative stones are equalled by free forms in the total pieces. Gold has been a foil for some of his finest work. One lovely piece pitted wood against narrow, long turquoise channel, and, on the opposite side, shell beads. Coral, jet, shell, and turquoise in vari-sized rectangles may jut upwards in uneven manner, like a city skyline, from silver bands which form the bracelet proper. Or, again, a bow guard is made of slim silver which outlines massive wooden pieces which, in turn, border a line of a few long coral pieces backed up by squares and irregular rectangles of turquoise, jet, and shell. A four-strand chunk turquoise necklace has a pendant of pearls with suspended chunks of coral and turquoise, the old and the new meeting in this sophisticated piece.

Traditional and new jewelry styles and creativity also are fused in the work of Preston Monongye. His pieces run the gamut from a heavy silver bracelet set with a central band of inlay or mosaic of coral, shell, turquoise, and jet to a large free form pendant combining a huge silver leaf on one side, with almost bell-like silver pieces from which

Examples of turquoise from Sonora, Mexico (Copper Plum Mine) and several objects crafted by Charles Loloma, Hopi. Top left is a wooden ring set with Battle Mountain turquoise. Top right is a gold bracelet with exterior Landers Blue stones while the inside is set with turquoise, lapis, and abalone. Blue Wind turquoise ornaments the central gold ring and that in the lower right, while the stone in the gold ring (center bottom) is from Lone Mountain.

Ever surprising is the work of Charles Loloma, Hopi. Here he suspends pearls from Morenci chunk turquoise for a different necklace, or adds a few ostrich eggshell beads and lapis lazuli to turquoise and wood in an unusual bracelet (upper right). In a gold bracelet (center), wood and lapis are lightened up with a touch of ivory and turquoise.

Half-finished, this beautiful mudhead basket is the result of the artistry of Alberta Susenkewa.

Hopi overlay bola ties by Lawrence Saufkie. The Kachina mask (left) is a favored Hopi theme; so too is the maze (right) borrowed from the Pima Indians.

Hopi overlay is here combined with more abundant turquoise, coral, and in several pieces, a bit of ironwood. The cast bracelet (lower right) is an attractive, unusual piece. Crafted by Duane Maktima.

emit graduated drops on the other, and both partially enclosing a large irregularly shaped turquoise. Certainly there are reminders of both Navajo and Zuñi silver craft in such modern pieces as this. Monongye may combine the traditional Hopi horned serpent or bear's claw with coral, jet, turquoise, and shell in a complete, non-Indian style.

To the mid-1970s, the demand for Hopi silver exceeded production. For a tribe which started out with silver crafting of no particular distinction, they have made great progress. Typical overlay, when well crafted, is distinctive. And certainly those Hopi individuals who have traveled new paths like Charles Loloma, are justly world-famous for their highly esthetic and original expressions in jewelry.

Deanne Sue Tewawina, a Second Mesa Hopi girl, wears the native hand-woven dress, coral and turquoise chunk-shell necklaces, the latter with an exceptionally long jacla. Her hair is done in the maidens' whorl style. Young girls are given kachina dolls so that they may become familiar with the costumes, masks, and body paint of these religious dancers.

Excellent examples of Hopi overlay craftsmanship. These bracelets show the great variety in design typical of the work of this tribe, from angular and curvilinear geometrics borrowed from their own rich ceramic background to a kachina mask, delightful flute players, bear paws, and a mythical bear swallowing a great arrow. Although little turquoise is used, here Lone Mountain is effectively and originally employed with the overlay silver work.

One of the best Hopi kachina doll carvers, Alvin James' dolls reveal fine modeling, great attention to detail, and excellent action. He is a true artist in every sense of the word. His dress and jewelry are typically Hopi.

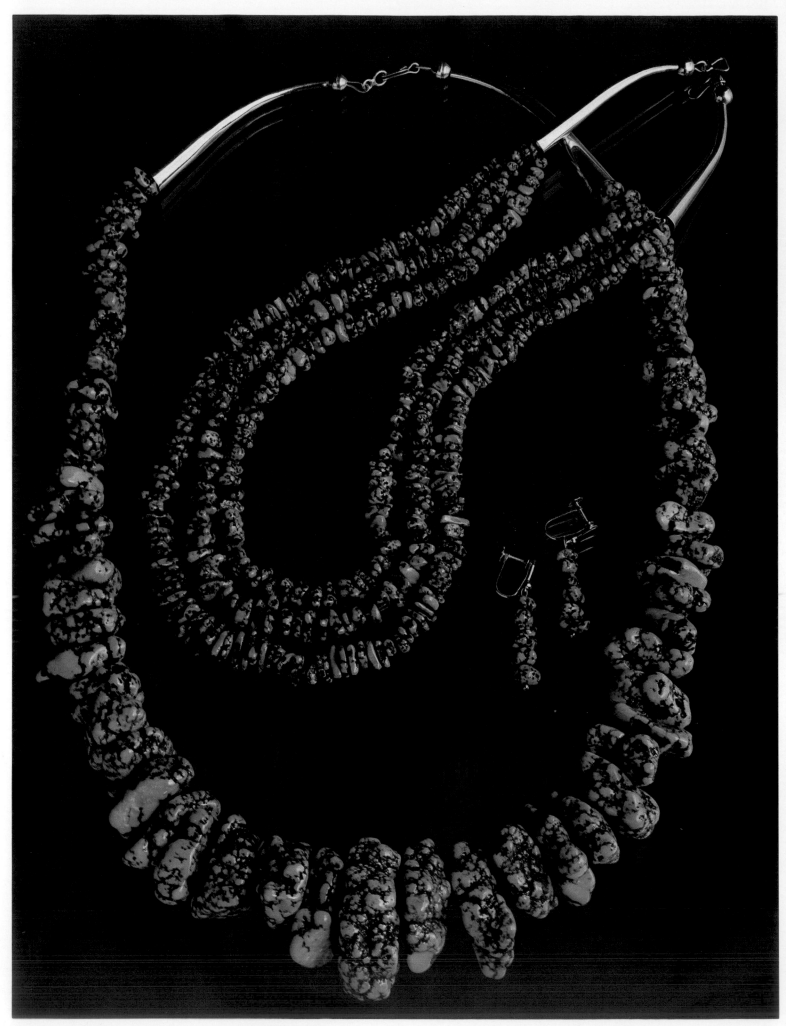

Morenci nuggets are used in both the smaller, three-strand and larger, single-strand necklaces and in the earrings. Gold fixtures add a finishing touch.

SANTO DOMINGO

"A Santo Domingo myth explains that when their people emerged from the underworld, two other groups of Pueblo peoples came with them, and that before they parted to go their individual ways, the Santo Domingos promised to make beads for the other Indians." So writes Bedinger.

And well should the making of objects of shell and turquoise be rooted in legend, for the two materials are deeply intertwined with myths; their continued popularity reflects their long lives. About two thousand years ago both materials were known to native Southwesterners, and never did the ancients lose sight of their beauty. Historic legend is so full of their presence that it cannot be doubted that both shell and turquoise were dear to the hearts of Southwestern pueblo Indians. This rich mythology is integrated into their religious beliefs also. Although not otherwise symbolic, generally speaking, and certainly not symbolic in pieces crafted for sale, nonetheless there are feelings in the hearts of many of the native wearers of turquoise and shell relative to their meanings.

The Santo Domingo puebloans are acknowledged top traders among all Southwestern Indians. Always they have managed to travel. Particularly fond of attending Navajo gatherings, nonetheless they are always to be seen at the Gallup Intertribal Indian Ceremonials, the Flagstaff Pow-Wow, and many another function such as ceremonies where large crowds gather and where they might participate in trade. Thus the Domingoans have been responsible for the wider distribution of certain types of Indian jewelry, and most particularly, turquoise and shell.

Modern Santo Domingo type necklace. Morenci nuggets are balanced by fluted beads. Coral and gold nuggets were combined in the smaller necklace.

Santo Domingoans have been getting turquoise from the mine at Los Cerrillos, fifteen miles from their village, for some time; unfortunately, most references say merely "for many years." One wonders how far back in time this means, for it is known that Los Cerrillos mines were worked prehistorically. To this source have been added turquoise from other mines worked by white men. The Santo Domingo Indian obtained quantities of the blue stone, converted much of it into beads, and traded them to other Indians, most particularly to Navajos, for they wanted the silver work produced by this tribe. Raw turquoise was traded to the Zuñis by the Domingoans as early as about 1890; polished turquoise beads were not taken to Zuñi until around 1920, this after the Colorado and Nevada mines were worked. These Zuñi dates are probably applicable to Santo Domingo-Navajo trade as well, although there is the possibility of earlier contacts between these two tribes. The Santo Domingo Indians have continued to go to Zuñi, often at the time of the Shalako ceremony. Later they added mosaic to their trade items for this pueblo.

Despite much contact with the Navajos, and brisk trade for silver with them, a Santo Domingo Indian learned silver crafting from a white man in Santa Fe. Presumably this occurred about 1893. This is also interesting in the light of the reference to Bourke's presence in Santo Domingo in 1881 at which time he obtained a Navajo crescent pendant within this village. Interesting, too, is the fact that the silver work at Santo Domingo was in the Navajo tradition. Most of the women in the village wore necklaces made of silver beads, with pendants in the form of crosses. These were probably of pueblo workmanship rather than Navajo; the style in question was often made at Laguna and Isleta. The concensus is that they were not made at Santo Domingo. There were never many smiths at Domingo, for their first love—shell and turquoise bead making—claimed their major interests. Adair reported that about 1940 there were seven smiths in the village, and about nine more plying this craft outside the pueblo. These men crafted silver primarily for their own people but did take some into Santa Fe and Albuquerque to sell. Admittedly they used better stones in heavier pieces for their own tribesmen.

An incident of interest occurred about this time, 1940. At the Santa Fe Indian School, the head of the arts and crafts division appealed to Kenneth Chapman to aid in adapting Santo Domingo pottery designs to use on dies for stamping their silver. The result was effective. Adair notes simple flat bracelets ornamented with delicately carved leaf patterns, a dominant theme in Santo Domingo pottery decoration. In addition to stamping, some overlay work was also done. A few cut-out pieces were also made, some in the forms of the roadrunner and other birds, another motif which was also borrowed from the ceramics of this pueblo. Bedinger, incidentally, related that after World War II smiths at Santo Domingo were still "decorating bracelets, brooches, and buttons with designs from their ancient pottery." Apparently this experiment was never developed to any extent; in fact, pieces made at this time are rarely seen in later years.

It was reported that some silverwork continued to be produced at Santo Domingo in 1950. In fact, Mimbres designs were added about this time. This trend did not last either. In fact, silver work, including both cast and hammered styles, was largely in the Navajo tradition as made at Domingo through the years and into the 1970s. Never was any quantity produced in these later years.

One interesting tale is told relative to Santo Domingo silversmithing, perhaps indicating that it may have been a tenuous expression, and this despite the fact that Adair notes that Santo Domingo was the only eastern village producing silver of any importance in 1940. He relates

that it was customary for small models of animals, both wild and domestic, and produce of the field to be made of clay and placed before the altar of the mission church, there to receive blessings at Christmas time. This ensured increase of animals and fruits of the fields. It seems that the tools of the smith and bits of silver were also placed in front of the altar for a comparable blessing.

Despite their efforts in silver, Santo Domingo Indians have been primarily workers in turquoise and shell, using a relatively limited amount of bone, jet, coral, and a few other materials. In the mid-1970s this list of materials was expanded, for a wide variety of shells was imported from many parts of the world. Color in particular became endless. Certainly the traditional craft of the Domingoans was and is turquoise and shell beads, plus more limited amounts of mosaic.

Mosaic has been important to this tribe for a long time. Earlier, simple inlay of turquoise alone or turquoise and jet might appear on a large shell or on pieces of shell. The shell was cut into a disc-shaped or oval pendant which was inlaid around the edge with turquoise. This inlay sometimes resembled a naja in form. Similarly shaped pendants were formed of old phonograph records. Bone was a common substitute for shell in the late 1920s and 1930s. Often pieces of this type were composed of fairly long and rounded bone fragments, almost oblong, with the smaller end drilled for stringing. The oval pieces were also set with turquoise, usually on their outer ends. Bone or wood or phonograph record fragments were sometimes substituted for the shell in these forms as in the rounded pendants.

Another piece made in mosaic was a whole shell with the upper or lower portion covered with tiny turquoises and the entire area bordered with a band of jet or jet and coral. Some of these pieces were well made, while others sometimes employed bits of phonograph records for the black. It might be added, too, that some of the coral was replaced by plastic, particularly in later years.

Drilling of beads prehistorically may well have been done with a simple hand-pump drill. Historically the same was used: a vertical shaft was balanced by a disc or flywheel of stone or pottery placed about two-thirds of the way down the shaft. Two buckskin thongs run from the top of the shaft to suspend a horizontal stick just above the disc; the shaft passes through a hole in the center of this stick. By manipulating this affair, the spinning of the shaft with a metal point is set in motion. Usually a bead is drilled from each side. Long after electricity was introduced, this hand pump remained popular, for there was less breakage in making beads.

In the late 1920s and 1930s, and continuing for decades, the following earring and necklace forms enjoyed renewed favor at Santo Domingo. Earrings which may have been popular prehistorically and into historic years involved a string of plain turquoise beads, or these with a few pink shell beads at the bottom. Some of these were short, some reached to the shoulders. Necklaces were more varied for they included a great variety of combinations. Plain turquoise or shell disc beads of single or multiple strands are called "heishi"; originally the term was applied to shell alone. These were popular into the seventies with fine craftsmanship featured in the best pieces in later years. Too, treated turquoise became popular in the late sixties and seventies, for the treated stone does not break as readily as the untreated.

Sometimes small or large and vari-colored beads were added to these necklaces, or a few "chunk" beads of turquoise might be inserted here and there. Perhaps the most favored of all necklaces, particularly by the Navajos and

Santo Domingo necklaces were sometimes graduated (top center).
Often, they were combined with metal, either regular beads of gold
or silver, or of liquid silver. Again, various materials and colors are
combined in a single necklace.

puebloans, was a style with a number of turquoise chunks distributed between clusters of disc turquoise or shell beads. Often the turquoise chunks were graduated. These, too, were usually in multiple strands. Suspended at the bottom of many of these necklaces were several short strands of beads which resembled the above-described earrings. These pieces are called "jaclas," and, as a matter of fact, it is believed that at least some jaclas were originally earrings. In the 1940s tortoise shell was introduced by a trader to Zuñi; often they used this in mosaic, and both Zuñis and Domingoans used it in heishi.

Perhaps the greatest change in necklaces which has occurred, and especially in the late 1960s and into the 1970s, has been the substitution of new types of beads for turquoise and grey, white, and pink shell. These include a multitude of shells of many colors, the types traded in from around the world. They are strung in a variety of ways, with a few or many inserted along with the native heishi, or with the imported shells of one or many colors, in single

or multiple strands, and in choker or longer fashion.

One last expression in jewelry made by the Santo Domingo Indians is the carving of so-called fetishes for necklaces. A true fetish is imbued with power and is of religious significance to these and other pueblo Indians. Generally, a real fetish is larger in size than the pieces in necklaces. Let it be said, then, that the term "fetish neck-lace" simply refers to a generalized bird or animal motif, and there is no symbolism involved in the necklace pieces.

For years the Santo Domingoans and the Zuñi Indians have carved small figures of birds, bears, and a few other animals of generalized nature and have incorporated them with heishi into necklaces. Coral, jet, shell of many colors, turquoise, serpentine, and rarely other materials are used. Craftsmanship varies tremendously, with some creatures extremely generalized in their carving, while others are beautifully made, even to incising to represent wings, insets for eyes, and other details. Individual craftsmen have become justly famous for their outstanding fetishes.

Happy and Willie Cly, two Navajos from Monument Valley. Colorful Navajo Indians have long lived among the equally colorful rock spires of Monument Valley. Jewelry worn by both Happy and Willie is of Santo Domingo style.

Right: Santo Domingo necklaces. The four strings on the left feature white shell disc beads with larger turquoise disc beads or chunks of the blue stone. Colored shell disc beads were also combined with chunk turquoise (top right), or just plain turquoise disc beads were made into multiple-strand necklaces (lower right).

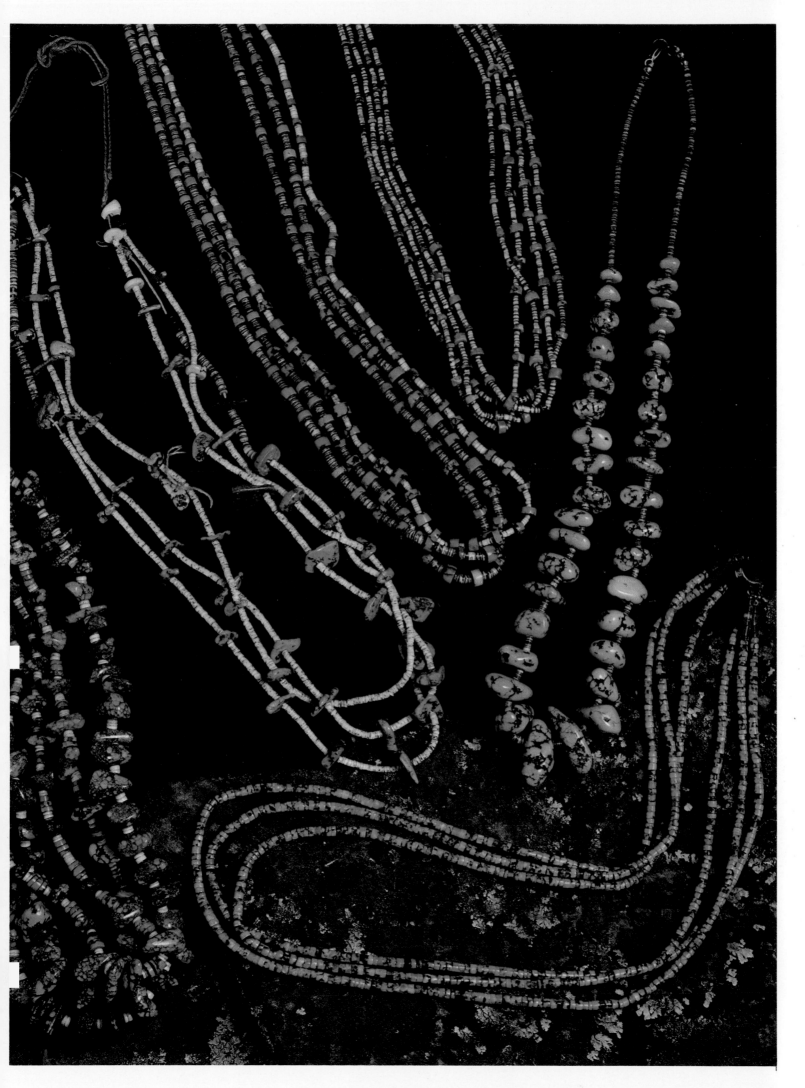

Although Navajo in style, this necklace was made by a Santo Domingo Indian. Simple file marks in the element surrounding the bezels set off the lovely, free-form turquoise.

Quite an exotic Santo Domingo necklace is crafted in this combination of traditional beads and jacla with the addition of elaborate turquoise and silver claws. Stabilized turquoise is often used when carving is done.

An array of contemporary Santo Domingo choker necklaces. Although several colors and materials have been combined in a single piece since pre-Columbian times, never has there been so much variety as now. Here are represented both natural and treated turquoise, several types of sea shells, tortoise shell, jet, serpentine, and silver.

Right: Recent trends in Santo Domingo necklaces have been in the addition of more basic materials and in combinations of more materials and/or colors in a single necklace. In the upper right are turquoise and pinshell, below this gold and the right graduated color in pinshell. Top center is a combination of jet and shell, and to the left, top to bottom: turquoise, vari-colored shell, coral and jet; pinshell, ivory and turquoise; and pinshell and turquoise.

Designed by Frank Patania is the bracelet (above) and the "yucca" ring (below left) . The spray of Burnham turquoise in the bracelet is balanced by the open metal work. Designed by Patania and crafted by a Navajo, the beauty of Burnham turquoise is again handsomely displayed in a spray style necklace, offset with leaves and rows of tiny drops of metal.

Frank Patania

A goldsmith apprenticeship in his homeland — Sicily — at the amazing age of six to ten years, served as a first firm foundation stone upon which the brilliant career of Frank Patania was built. After World War I, young Frank became designer and producer of sample jewelry for Goldsmith and Stern, New York City. Ill health took him to Santa Fe, New Mexico, in 1924, where a spell was cast upon him by the splendor of the Southwest and the beauty of Indian silver and turquoise. Three years later he established his own business in Santa Fe, ten years thereafter in Tucson, Arizona. With this rich background of training, inspiration, and accomplishment, Frank Patania became the first and the greatest non-Indian creator of turquoise and silver jewelry in the Southwest.

True artist that he was, Patania's genius supported his creativity. Into silver and turquoise he breathed the blessing of his love for the Southwest. Teaching silver craftsmanship to the Indian and learning from him at the same time, Frank's well of inspiration never ran dry. Thus was born a new and fresh beauty, manifested in sheerest simplicity to intricate design through the ever-fruitful meeting of turquoise and silver, in the capable and inspired hands of Frank Patania.

Appropriately, he has been called the Cellini of the Southwest.

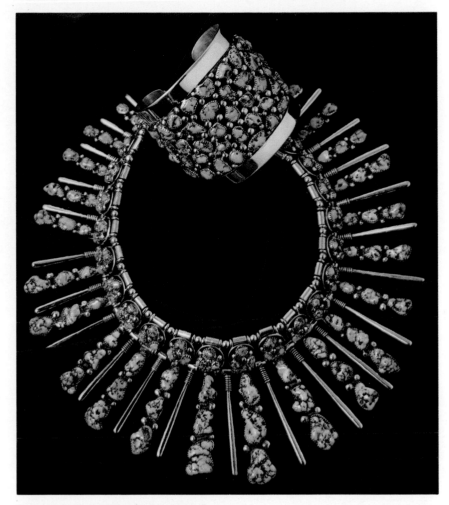

Both necklace and bracelet are set with Burnham nugget turquoise. The elegance imparted in Frank Patania's design was carefully crafted by an experienced Navajo silversmith.

Three typical Patania designs. Two necklaces and a bracelet show an extravagant use of turquoise, yet the carefully-matched color of stones, the studied form, and the handling of silver combine to make each a thing of beauty.

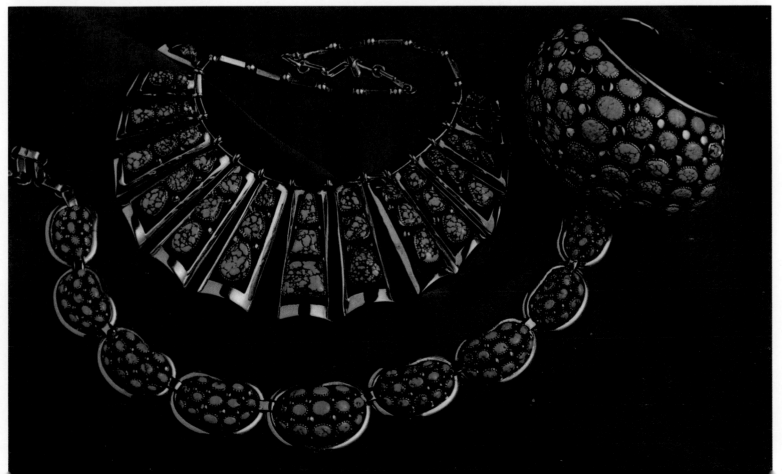

Clean, precise, and esthetically beautiful crafting characterize the work in this box, bracelet, and pendant by Frank Patania, Jr. Persian turquoise and a deep red coral add richness to each piece.

Frank Patania, Jr., is an outstanding craftsman in his own right. He has done remarkable pieces of architectural art, such as massive crosses in churches. His designing in jewelry is equally artistic, as illustrated here in a modern "watermelon" tourmaline set necklace and in two pieces in more traditional turquoise and silver in a cross and bracelet. The turquoise is Persian.

Special thanks to the Gallup Intertribal Indian Ceremonial Committee, its president Marlin Aitson, and Members George Hight and Earl Vance.

Right: Curley Moustache and friend Hosteen Begay Number Two. (These are the closest names we could obtain as neither spoke English and we no Navajo.) Two great faces reflecting the past but young enough to enjoy the Navajo Fair parade. Both were walking along together using a single walking stick to steady themselves.

"OLD PAWN"

Joe Ben Wheat, Curator of Anthropology, University of Colorado Museum, Boulder, Colorado.

"Old Pawn" is a term that, over the years, has meant many things to many persons. Today it is essentially a term used by collectors and traders or dealers in old Navajo and other kinds of Southwestern Indian jewelry. In earlier days, "Old Pawn" was exactly that — old jewelry pawned by the Indian who owned it, and sold by the trader when it went unredeemed. But today not all "Old Pawn" is old, and some of it has never been in pawn. Yet, the term "Old Pawn" has a compelling force about it, for when it accurately describes the article, it usually denotes a piece made by a native silversmith for his own people, worn by an Indian who treasured it, and finally brought into the market by the pawn system. It reflects native ideals of beauty, of craftsmanship, of tradition, and of intrinsic worth. It is this aura of antiqueness and genuineness that lends a magic to "Old Pawn." To the aficionado of "Old Pawn," the exquisite, often exuberant, and valuable Indian jewelry produced by today's artists somehow seems alien, not quite Indian, and so he searches for the simple jewels of the past.

The pawn system was essentially a Navajo phenomenon. It was the means by which old jewelry was brought into the collector's market. The system probably began with the first licensed traders on the Navajo Reservation. Silversmithing was new when the tribe returned from their four years of internment at Bosque Redondo, to a reservation set aside for them in their old homeland. They still had a few horses and cattle, and "Washington" — the U.S. Government — had issued sheep to rebuild their flocks to make them self-sufficient in food and in wool for weaving. But these were "soft" goods, and the "hard" goods — silver and turquoise, shell and coral — which they had previously obtained from the Spanish and Mexican *plateros*, or silversmiths, or from neighboring Pueblos, were scarce items.

With their recently-acquired skill in metal-working, they began to produce for themselves the articles of adornment that they cherished. Since most business transactions in the early trading posts consisted of barter and exchange, money, as such, meant little, but silver to convert into "hard" goods meant a great deal. Silver was not a common commodity on the Reservation in the 1870s, but when a smith acquired enough American silver coins, or, after about 1890, Mexican *pesos*, he would hammer them out, or melt them, and cast the silver into jewelry that he could wear or exchange, or, if necessary, use as security for a loan.

By the 1880s, the pawn system was a recognized part of Navajo economics. Pawn records of the late 1800s and early 1900s show that almost anything of value — guns, saddles, blankets, buckskins, and even buffalo robes — could be pawned, but most common was jewelry. Pawn moved in and out of the trading post in a fairly regular order. The pawn racks were heavily laden with a glittering assortment of "hard" goods in April, May, and June, but tapered off during July and August, and were lightest from September through December. By January, the build-up was again under way. This was because, with minor exceptions, Navajo income depended upon sheep. In late spring, the sheep were sheared, and wool not kept for weaving was sold to the trader, at which time the Navajo was expected to redeem his pawn. Late summer and through the fall was the season of the great Navajo ceremonial sings and social dances, so, in order to appear at his best, the Navajo made every effort to keep his jewelry and accouterments during that period. In late fall, he sold the summer crop of lambs to the trader, and this income helped carry him through the early winter. By late December, however, the Navajo had to resort to credit to buy food and clothing, and so, once again his jewelry had to be pawned to secure his credit. Besides, there were few occasions during the long, cold winter when he needed his finery. Although most traders made every effort to hold the pawn for the Indian who had pawned it, if it went too long unredeemed, eventually the trader might sell this "dead" pawn.

Nearly all of this early jewelry was made by the Navajo for his own use. Bracelets and rings were the most common items, but silver beads, plain or with "squash blossoms" and naja crescent, "ketohs" or bow guards, silver concha belts, silver buttons, and silver-mounted bridles followed closely in popularity, depending on the wealth of the individual. Most of this jewelry was relatively simple, decorated by filing, chisel-work, and simple tooling with hand-made punches. A few of these early pieces were set with turquoise, but most depended on the soft sheen of the silver for their effectiveness. Most of the turquoise available at the time tended to be greenish in color, but fine blue stones are sometimes found. Occasionally, native garnets, peridots, or bits of abalone shell were set instead of turquoise. Often, old pendants were reused for sets. Most stones tended to be flat, although occasionally a high-domed, hand-polished cabachon was set. The bezels in these early pieces were hammered out of coin silver and were relatively crude, often flush with or merely overlapping the edges of the stone, or with large, irregularly filed serrations holding the base of the cabachon. Cast pieces were generally somewhat irregular in plan, and the silver was often slightly pitted. These pieces were filed down and finished as smoothly as the smith could do it. Hollow silver buttons and beads, made by pounding small coins into a home-made die, were of various shapes, but all tended to be irregular in shape and were almost never exactly the same size. Great care was taken to remove the traces that it was once a coin, but occasionally some evidence of the edge-milling remains on the edge of a piece.

Besides the bracelets, rings, squash blossom necklaces, ketohs, belts, and bridles, the Navajo made a few other objects so rare today that many collectors have never seen a real one. These include powder-chargers for their muzzle-loading guns, tobacco canteens, tweezers, silver-mounted pouches worn by the Navajo in lieu of pants pockets, and mother-in-law bells to warn the Navajo male that his wife's mother was in dangerous proximity.

White shell and turquoise bead necklaces go back into prehistoric times in the Southwest, and coral and glass trade beads were brought by the Spanish at least by 1750. The Navajo had a fair share of these beads, to which they added earrings composed of short loops of turquoise beads. These earrings, called "jaclohs," were hung over the bottom of the necklace when not being worn and were frequently pawned at the same time as the necklace. These early mixed necklaces had moderately large white disk beads and smoothly finished turquoise pendants. Most of the early coral beads were small and rounded, but long, tubular coral made its appearance by the 1880s. All of these necklaces were composed of as many strands as the owner could afford.

The turn of the century saw a number of changes in the jewelry destined to become "Old Pawn." One important change was the introduction of high-quality turquoise in quantity, much of it from newly opened commercial mines in Nevada. Most of these stones were hand-cut at the mines, and included both cabachons and shaped flat stones. Hundreds of small, round cabachons, known as "snake eyes," were cut from the small pieces left over, and immediately became popular, especially around Ganado. But the major change was the quickening of the curio trade. Navajo silver was heavy, but the new "tourist" silver was much lighter. What it lacked in weight it made up for in decorative stamping. The traders introduced such "Indian" symbols as swastikas, thunderbirds, and arrows. Watch fobs, stick pins, and silver teaspoons became tourist souvenirs, but some of the bracelets and rings remained in Navajo hands, found their way onto the pawn racks, and have become respectable "Old Pawn." For their own use, the Navajo continued to make silver bridles, ketohs, squash blossom necklaces, and concha belts, but all tended to become more ornately decorated with a greater use of turquoise. Closed conchas with repoussé centers, butterflies, and ornate buckles became more popular, largely replacing the plain open-center conchas. Silver hatbands started shortly after 1900, and when the black, high-crowned Navajo hat came in, about 1915, they became common. Dress ornaments such as fancy buttons, brooches, and collar points were introduced.

Sheet silver was introduced in the 1920s and gradually tended to replace the old hammered silver. Many of the bracelets, ketohs, and rings superficially looked like the old silver, but their lighter weight and mechanically smooth surfaces seem to lack the sensuous appeal of the hand-made silver. With sheet silver came commercial bezel stock and a wide variety of commercial silver wires. It was no longer necessary to pound out the silver, heat it, and pull it through a wire block. One result was that much of the silver of the period had a uniformity and mechanical perfection lacking in the earlier work. Turquoise began to appear in the form of flattish, irregular nuggets, and, combined with tan shell beads called "heishi," from the Pueblos, gave birth to the turquoise nugget necklace that gradually replaced the older white shell and smoothed turquoise pendants. More and more, tubular coral beads replaced the smaller, earlier beads.

Another trend of the twenties was the increasing use of Zuñi jewelry by the Navajo. Early Zuñi silver was so similar to Navajo that it is difficult to distinguish, but the Zuñis have been lapidaries since prehistoric times, and their jewelry came more and more to feature turquoise. Silver became simply a vehicle to carry the stones. Clusters and rows of turquoise, as well as mosaics of shell, jet, coral, and turquoise, became the hallmark of Zuñi work. Not only did the Navajo acquire quantities of Zuñi jewelry, but they began to make jewelry in the Zuñi style, and ere long, these pieces—bracelets, rings, dress ornaments, and massive, turquoise-laden necklaces derived from the old squash blossom motif—began to hang from the pawn racks in the Navajo trading posts.

The two decades between 1920 and 1940 were the heyday for collectors of "Old Pawn." The Navajo were not immune to the changing tides of fashion. Simple old silver went out of style, and often the Navajo would let his pawn go dead. Sometimes he would buy jewelry of newer kinds, and by tacit understanding, the trader, after the legal time limit had expired, would sell this pawn. Often it went for the amount of the pawn plus a legal 10 percent charge. Occasionally other Indians would buy it, but in order to avoid harsh feelings among the local inhabitants, most of it was sold to the collectors who braved the dirt and gravel roads to the trading posts, or to curio dealers. Thus did the fine old jewelry of the past and the newer articles of ever-changing fashion pass from the Navajo to the collectors of "Old Pawn."

World War II marked the end of an epoch when the pawn system was an integral part of Navajo economics. With increasing wage-work, the passing of the slow, horse-drawn wagon, and its replacement by the omnipresent "pickup," and the opening of the Reservation, the Navajo began to move to a cash economy. The pawn rack became less and less important in all except the remotest parts of the Reservation. In some posts there are still fine old pieces, but by and large, little of it leaves the post. The increase in value, spurred by the popularity of "Old Pawn," has caused the traders to hold it. Meanwhile, some of the mass-produced Indian jewelry turns up in shops and auctions with mass-produced pawn tickets. Some good copies, aged to look like the old pieces, also appear on the market, and some of these are fine jewels in their own right.

"Old Pawn" has, in some ways, degenerated into a catch phrase, like "New and improved," to trap the unwary. Nevertheless, there still is good "Old Pawn" to be had. Old collections are broken up, and reliable dealers buy and sell them. Occasionally a few good, old pieces, bearing the patina of long and cherished wear, are found in the trading posts. Inevitably, the jewelry of today will become old, but with the changes in the pawn system and in the market, one suspects that it will become "Antique" and not "Old Pawn."

Right: Not a great deal of turquoise was used in Navajo jewelry until after the turn of the century, and even then it was secondary to the silver (two upper left). The Zuñis used more of the blue stone and also embellished pieces with fancier silver work, often reducing the squash blossom to a very small size or wiped it out entirely (second from bottom left, could be Zuñi).

Bridles and belts were among the early pieces of silver crafted by the Navajos; massive simplicity characterized the best, as seen in these pieces. Turquoise was not added until after 1880. Round conchas were earlier; oval ones later.

Lovely old Zuñi and Navajo style bracelets, with a cast Navajo bow guard in the center. Larger oval stones, often five of them, and graduated from a larger central one, or three stones, were typically Navajo, as the rosette style was typically Zuñi.

Photography by Naurice Koonce and Alan Manley

Ray Manley, in publishing this book, made the selection of subjects, both for the Indian portraits and the Indian-made jewelry.

It was with considerable satisfaction that two people very close to him were responsible for all the photography.

Alan is not only pursuing his father's lifetime career of photography but also that of his great-great grandfather who had a studio in Canton, Ohio, and was the official photographer to President McKinley.

Alan's friendly personality made it much easier for him to photograph over 150 Indians in preparation for the selection of the ones used. There were no refusals from any of the Indians approached, and this is quite an accomplishment. How would you react to a couple of strangers knocking on your door, asking you to come out into the sunshine for a photograph, and, if you didn't mind, wear your finest clothes and put on your best jewelry?

Naurice Koonce is a long-time friend and partner and an old hand at jewelry photography. Many of his arrangements have appeared in *Arizona Highways* and in Ray Manley's *Southwestern Indian Arts and Crafts.* All the photographs in *Turquoise, the Gem of the Century,* were done by Naurice. His photography of the C. G. Wallace collection and its publication in *Arizona Highways* was the first "public appearance" of this fine selection; it had been shown to private audiences only prior to this time.

Text by Clara Lee Tanner

Clara Lee Tanner became an Arizona resident at the early age of two or three years. Most of her education was in Tucson and at the University of Arizona, with additional graduate work at the Universities of Chicago and Mexico. Travel in Mexico and Europe supplemented her background for teaching. Her career began as an instructor in Anthropology 47 years ago at the University of Arizona where she is now Professor emeritus and continues teaching courses in Southwestern Indian Art in the Department of Anthropology.

Mrs. Tanner has had an active interest in Southwest Indian cultures and the arts and crafts of this area for more than 40 years. Her research and writing have been largely in these subjects. She has published more than 100 articles in professional journals and magazines, as well as four books — a fifth book is currently at press.

In 1936, Clara Lee married John F. Tanner. They have one daughter, Sandra, and two grandchildren. The Tanners have enjoyed sharing a mutual interest in Indian arts and crafts through his shop and her professional career.

For many years Mrs. Tanner has lectured throughout Arizona and occasionally in other states, again in the fields of Southwest Indians and their crafts and painting. She has also judged at state fairs, Indian art competitive exhibits, and Indian craft shows on many occasions.

Left: A medley of old Pawn! It includes plain, multiple-strand coral and shell disc bead, chunk turquoise necklaces, probably Santo Domingo crafted. There are open-center, plain silver belts, and bracelets made of turquoise mounted on cast triangular silver pieces — both old Navajo styles. And tucked in the lower left corner is an old-style Navajo ring, a large square turquoise with four simple silver drops on each side.

Back cover: Monument Valley, northern Arizona, is marked by many and varied formations which wind and weather have carved from the great sandstone deposits of this area. Among them are these Totem Poles, the most slender of all the carved rocks. As Fred Harvey influenced the Navajo and the Hopi into making rugs and pottery that would sell, contemporary traders and style-conscious silversmiths have turned to gold and unusual modifications of older styles. Here the claw and fine Burnham turquoise are mounted in gold.